My life with Kundalini

By

Lotte Søs Farran-Lee

My life with kundalini
© Lotte Søs Farran-Lee 2017
Lotte Søs Farran-Lee have the rights as authors of this book.
All rights reserved, including the right to reproduce this book or portions thereof in any form whatsoever, without prior permission from the publisher except for short quotations used in reviews.The material contained in this book is for reference purposes only, and is not intended as a substitute for counselling, or other medical and/or therapeutic services

1. edition 1. print 2017
isbn 978-87-998430-5-3
Published by Human Publishing Worldwide ApS
www.humanpublishing.com
Email: info@humanpublishing.com

MY LIFE WITH KUNDALINI

Copyright 2017 by Lotte Søs Farran-Le

All rights reserved. No part of this book may be used or reproduced in any manner whatsoever without written permission from Lotte Søs Farran-Lee.

The scanning, uploading and distribution of this book via the Internet or via any other means without the permission of the publisher is illegal and punishable by law.

First Printing: august 2017

Table of Contents

CHAPTER 1
The search... 5

CHAPTER 2
Meeting my life energy........................ 17

CHAPTER 3
The man and the woman 27

CHAPTER 4
Awakening... 37

CHAPTER 5
Shutting down....................................... 47

CHAPTER 6
The helping people arrive 53

CHAPTER 7
The tantric world 63

CHAPTER 8
My Italian angel.................................... 73

CHAPTER 9
I am coming home............................... 83

CHAPTER 10
Wrapping up... 89

CHAPTER 1

The search

Welcome to my world

Can you start a book with, "I really do not want to write this book"? Maybe not. Nevertheless, that is what I do, but, on the other hand, I do want to write this book because I have something at heart to tell - but truly, I would wish that the subject were not kundalini.

First of all, I am not an enlightened guru, a yoga teacher. I have not studied Buddhism and not gone to India - I love Italy. I am not a meditation teacher, etc.

Secondly, I am not here to tell you or debate with you whether kundalini is a phenomenon, a myth of old ancient history, if it is real, if it is a state that can be scientifically proven, if it is a way to gain enlightenment if you do it in a specific way. It is not a book based on facts from watching and teaching the energy called kundalini and the old wisdom of it.

It is a book written by me who has had and still has the experience of living with a full-blown kundalini since 2004 where I turned 32. When you say "kundalini" to people, the reaction goes from *oh, better get away from this one; this can be very dangerous,* or *how lucky you are!* This is just a fine energy that runs through the spine so blissfully.

"I went to a mental institution, and many do." *"You can go crazy."* *"You just have to do it."* *"It is just your attitude."* *"It is not supposed to happen this way."* *"That does not exist."* *"You need to have a guru."* *"It is a beautiful energy, and really everyone has their eyes on it, and that is the way it should be."*

The thing is this. What do you do when it happens and you are not surrounded by people who know anything about it? You are scared to go to doctors; they will probably just think you are crazy. There is no guru around the corner of a 7/11. You intuitively know that it happened but just do not know what to do or scared of getting in the wrong hands.

I am not alone with this - that I know - and I also know that for all of us who go through this, it is real, and it is *very* real. I also know for that amount of people who go through this, just as many different experiences are what this is and how it is.

This book is about the energy, kundalini, that suddenly entered my life and the journey of the spontaneous energy that turned into everything I just had and have to take care of in my life. There is a lot of discipline to this.

It is not going to be a pretty book in the sense that I write about how beautiful this energy is, because many times I do not think it has been at all as beautiful and blissful as people say. Many times, I would have sold it if I could, selling it to someone who wished all their life to get it, and basically, they could get it for free.

At the same time, this is also a love story in cleansing and healing me, learning the tenderness, love, breath, sensitivity, sensuality, sexuality, lust and strength and wisdom that was in me just waiting to blossom.

Really, all kunda (as I call her, because it makes her soft and bold) wanted me to do was to live my soul. Her job is just to bring me forward all the time, and once she forced me, I have resisted so much and been full of anxiety where she would lead me. The hardest part is to trust her and be completely willing to surrender to her, living her will, and hence living the will of me, of what I already am.

The journey of kundalini has been very sexual. I know that kundalini is our life energy and hence also our sexual energy, but this matter has been the part that has been so profound in me and for many years didn't know what to do with this energy.

This subject is touched slightly in many of the books written about kundalini. In tantric books, it is a natural thing where the sexual energy is used to bring in higher consciousness and open the heart. Or the books write about the energy where it truly can experience blissful sex reaching a higher consciousness together with making love and have the feeling of merging together. But for me it has filled everything in life, so much that it became that which controlled me.

When it comes to kundalini and sex, it also comes to kundalini and love, and my quest for love has been huge. I wanted to feel and know what love was because I intuitively knew that if I could love unconditionally, I could free myself.

I have had many questions of which I may have asked too many, I know, and I have also talked with many people about sex and love, and these conversations have taken me far and wide, have made me meet wonderful people with beautiful hearts and the courage to talk, and hence, those people have been a part of my journey and I have been a part of theirs.

When tantra entered my life, I met an entity and a basic philosophy which started a very healing process for me, uniting sex, love, kundalini and body, and hence, tantra will be a part of the book because it has healed me so much.

In this book I will write about my journey and why it has been so healing in regard to my kundalini rising. It took me more than six years after my spontaneous rising to find the people with the heart and the courage to help me on the way to an understanding of this energy, what it is to me and how to support and nourish it in my life.

It has been truly amazing how people and countries have helped, and still do, in order for me to find more and more peace and joy with my dear kundalini. And then, on top of that, an angel arrived in the midst of all the mess and helped heal my heart and soul.

I hope you will enjoy this journey of mine, getting behind the scenes and get kundalini down on the ground from the heavens she is coming from. It will be raw, bitter and sweet, splashed with love, tears and laughter.

It is very nice to meet you.

Landing in life

So here I am, brand new in this world. I am going back a bit – quite a lot, actually. I go back to the day I was born because, basically, landing in life gives you this huge question: "Who am I?" But do you really need to answer that? I'm not so sure anymore, because the more I travel through life, the more I understand that this can never be answered. The only thing that is, is change.

Here I am. I am born. Just to give you a rough idea of who I am in that respect, not from my soul, not a big philosophic question but more in a very square way. I was this child who, since I was born, always felt as if I had been born into the wrong family and in the wrong country. I felt I didn't belong.

I was a very sensitive and reserved girl with a lot of anxiety. I could sit in the window, looking out, and just be daydreaming, watching things go by and think, "What are people doing here? What am *I* doing here?"

I lived in my daydream world and I muddled through by being very good in school and doing my things. I knew I just had to do my things, so I looked to other people and copied what they did to the best of my ability in order to get the sense of it, but I never told anyone about my inner world, about how rich it was in so many ways no one ever dreamt about.

I had a lot of emotions as a child. I could lie in my bed at night, for instance, and it was as if anything could get very big and get very small and I had this bodily feeling that I was not real, and at times, conversely, I felt spacious. I never told anyone about all these feelings and my anxiety concerning this.

In many ways, I was very silent because I felt that no one would understand if I told them who I was. Basically, I kept all my gifts of who I was inside.

CHAPTER 1 • THE SEARCH

Pain

On the whole, I felt so different and in a way I felt so lost. But it was really more like a deep pain about being alive that started to grow. I had a lot of anxieties about many things, and I was scared that the outer world would take away my inner world; that the outer world would become stronger and truer than my inner truth, so I shut down more and more, and isolated myself.

I was very hard on myself because I felt so different and I didn't want anyone to see that I was different, so I was hiding. In all this hiding, my pain of life started really to grow.

But my will was strong and I wanted to learn, so I kept copying what people did because I thought that it might make me happy. I decided that if I did what other people did when they looked happy, then that it would lead me to happiness.

There was just one catch… it didn't.

Teach me how to live

The more I grew up, the more I was in pain. I was really in pain about being alive at all. I got really dark and had so many thoughts about life, and I just wanted to know what this was all about. How could I create a happy life for myself?

When I was looking around, it seemed that everybody knew what they wanted, and I sort of bought into those truths, but I didn't really know why. People knew what they were doing and everybody was talking about having some bigger goal in life. It seemed to me that everyone knew what it was, and then they just went for it.

It seemed as if they got the right education from the beginning and they got the right jobs, and I felt I was lagging behind. As if everyone had been given a manual on life, with some basic information in it, and I just hadn't received such a book at birth. At the same time, I just carried on and did the things I was supposed to do; I didn't quit, but I felt that this pain was growing and the darkness was taking up still more space.

All I wanted to know was what to do with this life. Who could teach me to live? I went to the doctor at one point in my teenage years, and he wanted to give me this one solution that I really didn't believe in. Medicine.

Then I was lucky I met this woman. She was a therapist, and I was hungry to be taught how to live. The first time I went there, she looked at me and said, "You have got to take responsibility for your life. The ship has sailed. Your childhood is gone, things are done. You can't change that."

From that point, I started to attend a one-year seminar with her where we did a lot of exercises for body and mind. And when I began that year, a new world started to open up for me. I met people who could understand having that pain and I felt that now I had a place where I could start looking into all this pain and anxiety I was going through.

I felt that slowly, I was beginning to see the light.

You know, I could write pages up and down about that, but this is not why we are here in this book. I just want you to introduce you to my pain.

I want to be clean

Anyway…

In this seminar, I became very aware of wanting to be clean all the time. I had this inner search that every time I felt that I was being faced with a lie I had concocted about life, about myself, or about others, I wanted to clean it out. Hence, I started to become very honest about everything I saw, and I spoke out, verbalized it, because I really wanted to face it.

All the participants thought I had ever so much courage. The teacher often said to me that I was very honest, but for me, honesty was the only tool I had when facing my inner truth of who I was. If I lied or got stuck in some illusion about how life ought to be, I felt dirty and exposed, and I could not face that.

Whenever I could not face it and see it, I got more dirty again. When I got dirty, I felt very bad. I felt I got stuck and I felt all the anxiety of being in a space of stuck energy, like being stuck in mire. That was the worst part.

I went on that seminar when I was 25. I started really beginning to learn how to live cleanly, and this part was not just done overnight, but I felt the importance of eating good, clean food and I started to have this cleansing need all the time.

I wanted to clean off my emotional dirt. I needed to stop smoking. I needed to exercise. I wanted to be clean, but mostly it was to find that inner truth I so deeply longed for.

What I didn't know at the time was that I was unaware how much this meant to me and how this would save my life. This feeling of being 100% clean is still important in my life and has helped to be where I am now. If I hadn't done that, I'm sure I had not ended up in a good place. And when I say I still live it, it is because I need to, I don't have a choice of living untruthfully to my soul.

I have often envied other people for being able to lie; lie to themselves, to others, and indeed to their life and soul. They could make decisions that would freak out their whole system.

The snake inmy body-mind

In this body-mind seminar which I attended, we did a lot of exercises in order to get information about how to get more conscious about ourselves. We did a lot of visualizations, too.

The one visualization which I will now share with you was one of the really big signs that started to show up in my life about what was coming.

At the seminar, we had this huge room with a wooden floor and our small mattresses, and we were asked to lie down on our mattresses. We were going on this visualization trip. We were going to close our eyes. We had to go into our inner forests. In our individual forest, we had to find our chakra animals.

In my forest I walked among a lot of trees. It was very dark because the trees were very, very tall, and at the same time I could see this light. There were all these bushes around me and the tall trees. It was a bit like a jungle and yet it was not a jungle. It was warm and just very, very nice.

I could hear the teacher's voice from far away: *Go out and find your first chakra, your root chakra animal.*

I went out and I looked into the bushes and I looked around me, and suddenly it was there. It was a snake. *What?* I looked at it, and I thought having a snake was really disgusting, because we were supposed to bring our animal inside us and start focusing on it, in our root chakra.

At that point, I was appalled at the thought of this curly snake moving around in my root chakra. At that time, I was really into the whole seminar. For me it was about grounding, so I just wished that my animal could have been a cow instead. For me, a cow was very grounded and much more agreeable than a snake.

Even though the instructor said we should keep the animal we found, I didn't listen. I thought a snake was too reprehensible, so I threw the snake into the bushes in my forest, and I decided that I wanted my cow.

I knew I was lying to myself. I *definitely* knew I was lying to myself, but I did it anyway. I kept my cow.

We went through all the chakras; we got out of the visualization and were lying down on the floor, and everything was fine.

Afterwards we went out for a break, and I heard all the other participants talking about their various animals. A lot of the others had been to many seminars before, so they knew a lot about chakras and about spiritual matters, but I had no clue about anything.

My only goal was to be happy, so we could have done anything, really. As long as I felt that it was helping me, it was good.

These other participants were talking a snake as a very fantastic thing to have in one's root chakra. I didn't know why, but I could hear it was good, and also that an eagle in the crown chakra would be fantastic. I have had that one too, so that was kind of cool ; I felt good about keeping my eagle.

But I felt the lie, the lie that I had just perpetrated by choosing the cow instead of the snake, and now that I learned that having a snake was kind of cool I thought I had to change this, so ...

I ate my lunch and then I went back to the room where we had the exercise. I lay down on my mattress. All the others were in the other room eating their lunches, but I went back into my forest, I walked back into my visualization and I knew I just had to find the snake again.

I found it again. I picked it up and I placed it in my root chakra again, and I felt it was the right thing to do. I didn't know why, but I knew the cow had been a lie.

Now I was here with my snake. I had no idea how much that snake would mean to me later on in life…

I became a seeker

When I attended that one-year body-mind seminar, something changed profoundly in me because I got so aware that I had to take responsibility of everything in me and in every aspect of my life.

This started a completely new way of thinking and outlook on life, because now I needed every interaction I was in, everything that happened to me, to mean something. It became a job, a mission. It was as if I were hired to be a seeker. It became a huge part of my everyday life.

I was constantly searching within myself and around me – I kept asking which kind of relationship I had with different people, what that revealed about myself, and how could I change it in me if it didn't serve me properly.

The hard part of this is that basically everything I did became wrong because it had to mean something. Everything had to mean something. If a little thing went wrong, I took a huge responsibility and felt that something greater had to be wrong with me because these small things didn't go the way I wanted them to.

It was very hard work. I analyzed everything I was in. The good thing was, however, that I really wanted to learn from my experiences so I could be clean all the time; I constantly sought to see myself with truthful eyes so I could live the life I felt I was here to live.

I was constantly arguing with myself, too. I was constantly changing all the time, because change meant that I was going somewhere. I felt I was getting closer and closer to the truth about who I was.

Nevertheless, I had no idea what I was seeking. I just felt this urge within myself. There was something that I knew could become so much better when I reached my undefined goal.

I also knew it would take some time, but I had this very deep urge within me, and I just knew that one day I would crack the puzzle.

This urge to find that answer within myself kept me in the role of the seeker of some inner truth. It made me go to workshops, go to talks, get an education, meet with people. I just wanted to see and learn who had found the key to happiness. What did other people do?

What I also saw most of the time was that I could never commit to one whole truth. If someone said, "this is a philosophy of life and this is the way you should do it," I always felt it to be partially true, but I never believed that one truth should become the only one.

Then there were all my expectations that came with it – the seeking business. All the expectations and hopes that things would get better. "I will get there one day, I will get to that goal and then everything will fall into place."

It was all about the struggle of getting to that goal I had set myself and my belief that when I got there, things would be great. But what was this "there"? and how could I get there and what would it mean? Was it a job? Was it a gateway to something greater?

I was still questioning things all the time, but all I knew was that I had to keep on looking, keep on looking at myself, keep on learning. That was my main purpose in life.

CHAPTER 1 • THE SEARCH

Looking back

Sitting here now, watching that part of my life and seeing it from the perspective of the journey I am going to tell you about in my book, I know that that journey was already given to me when I was born.

I can see now that I was already pre-wired to do this. A lot of the things I struggled with and all the pain I was going through as a child and a teenager and a young woman have helped me in never giving up and always staying on the track of something greater that would happen to me. I didn't give up even if I felt at times that it would have been the easiest thing by far.

I can see that I have spent so much of my time being someone I was not, and that I wished that I was born differently, had a different history, had different pains, different pleasures – but really, it is not possible and I think we all know that, but we sometimes wish it anyway.

In many ways, my history also led me to becoming a leader quite early in my life. Even though I struggled to become a leader, I had always made the choices I needed to make anyway.

Every time I tried to blame someone or something else, such as "I can't do it because of this and that," I always ended up doing it anyway because the urge to do it was always much stronger for me; even if it felt scary, unsafe, too much, too big, I always did it.

There was something in me always calling much more profoundly than anyone else's opinion.

Looking back from where I am now, I feel very humble about seeing my journey, step by step as it was, was in fact pre-ordained, and it is really beautiful to see that there has been a red thread in the mess, after all.

I had tried a lot to throw away this weirdness and specialness and feeling different, all these sights that I felt did not fit into the "normal way of thinking and being," but now, looking back, I can see that I had the pure goal from the beginning. I just taught myself to shut it down.

The purpose of this journey that you are on with me now in this book is to realize what my goal was about. I can see now that being a seeker was such a huge part of my identity that I was not really living my own life while I was clinging to this big illusion.

Being a seeker is an ambiguous thing but still a fantastic thing. It gives you hope. It kept me moving forward all the time, never ever giving up. I could see that in a way some parts of it had been an illusion, but also that it has fueled me on my journey and enabled me to get through it.

Meeting my life energy

Meeting the therapist

Life had moved on since my one-year body-mind seminar, and I was starting to become a therapist because I felt that there was something in that direction which I needed to do. Something deep inside me was telling me that I didn't know if I had to become a therapist, but that the journey there was very important to me.

At first, I had declined joining this therapist education, but then there was this deep voice within me saying that I just had to go. I just couldn't say no, even if becoming a therapist wasn't exactly a dream of mine.

So I started out, and during my training, we had to go to external therapists to clean our own history, and I did that. It was a fantastic thing for me because it really felt as if I was cleaning myself. We had lists, and I was looking down that list, and there was this one man on the top of it that was beaming out. It was the only name I could see.

I thought, "You have a lot of energy in that part, so go for that one." I called him up and I got an appointment to go to my first therapy session with him.

The first day I came too early because I am always so scared of being late. I sat down in a chair and I thought, "Here we go again. What are we looking at this time?" We sat down, and he was very different from anyone else because he was working with contact. He was actually working with what happened while I was sitting there in this chair with him.

This was the most provoking thing for me ever because I had become so skilled in all this processing work. I didn't mind processing every emotion. Every time there was a new process, I just went into it as if it was my job. I knew what I could do when I was angry and anxious and crying and happy and all these processes.

The way he worked was new because he was working with the contact of staying with a person and with what happened then and there, and I was terrified because that meant that I was being observed in this very moment, not my past but my present, and I had to be aware of what happened when I was actually in contact with someone.

Suddenly I could see that this was something I had tried to get out of all my life, and that I wasn't very good at being in contact with another person. As I said, I had tried all my life to observe other people, trying to see what they were doing, so I tried that, but it was not something that came from within me. I had no clue about being in contact and staying there. This was a very new thing for me.

After I had been there a couple of times, I was sitting in this chair, and an amazing thing happened: I was really looking forward to going to therapy every time.

Suddenly I became aware that while I was sitting in his chair, the energy, the thing that I had been looking for in all my life made sense, was around me. It was just present. He sat there, I sat there, and in the space between us, the energy that I was looking for came alive.

I was so confused. What is this? It was not something I could see. It was not *I want to do this specific thing in my life*. No, I wanted to learn the energy, and how can you learn an energy? *Excuse me, this is just a feeling I have inside, and this is really fantastic and I really want to learn this, but how do I do it?*

This is how it was. I started to think with my head because I wanted to learn this. This is what I want to do in life, I thought. This is what I have been looking for all my life, and I felt I had to learn it; I had to do it.

Some people said to me, "You can't do it," but I would always think, "No way I'm giving up. I'm not done here." I felt I had not even begun yet. So I didn't quit. I was being very stubborn because this was something I had wanted to do all my life, and this was in fact the first time I found something I truly wanted to do.

I just had to figure out what exactly it was I wanted to do because I was just sitting there anyway. I was in this wilderness within myself.

I had at that time learned that everything that happened in this room was a mirror of me, so I knew it had nothing to do with him. At the same time, things happened when I sat there.

I needed to come up with a clever idea to understand how I could get this information out.

I got really angry with this situation because I responded, "why does everything have to be like that for me?" Why can I not just be a hot dog vendor or something very simple? Why did I have to want to go and learn an energy? I just want a regular job, a regular life.

This was what I had been looking for all my life and it was so hard to explain to anyone, even myself, but I just knew it was right for me. From that moment, things started to turn into a real mess. I tried to control this mess, not for a short period but for a long time… I guess you can say, for the rest of my life, because I had not seen this coming.

I have a plan

I was sitting in this mess, and I wanted to be a bit constructive about it because I wished to learn this energy. I wanted to know what it was. I knew that if I could learn it, my plan was that I could take it and bring it out into my everyday reality and just simply implement it there. It sounded like a perfect plan.

In a way, I felt as if I knew he was a real person and I know I went to a real place called the therapist room, but at the same time, it was not a real room for me. It was not my real life. It was a place to practice. And it was room where I could take out my inner world and analyze it and wear it and feel it, and then, for me, it was supposed to bring about a transformation in that room so I could bring it out into my real world, and hence into my life.

For me, it was about getting the information between him and me out in that room because I knew I could not get him out of the room, and I didn't want that either.

However, at the same time, he became very important to me, and I didn't like him to become so important because then I felt I was attached and dependent on him for my life to work out, and I don't like to depend on someone.

This was what happened then… I could see that my therapist was a very important part of this puzzle. The thing was that I firmly believed that if only I needed a plan, I was sure to come up with an incredibly brilliant plan sooner or later.

I knew that every person who comes into your life, be it with a positive or a negative charge, can teach you something about yourself. You always benefit in some way from others. So this was my plan with my therapist then.

My plan was that if I used him as my mirror, I would be able to learn what this energy between us was all about. I had a plan. I must say, I believed I had it all figured out, and I thought I was really on top of things, and thought it would be easy because I could practice whenever I was in his therapy room.

So I made a decision. I imagined that if I let myself fall in love with him, I would be able to get all the projections out and then I would be able to know this energy, bring it back home to myself and hence… the job would be done. Everything would become better because then I learned what I wanted to do in my life.

Many plans just do not go the way you want them to. God is laughing when you are making plans, but this was what I had in mind. I had made a plan. And it just had to work…

Something has happened

Some time after my decision about falling in love with my therapist, something started to shift within me. It was very hard to put a finger on what it was, but I began to withdraw from life. I started to get into my inner world a lot, and I just felt very different from what I had been before.

I knew I had this plan, so I knew this love that I was looking at was not a real love. It was not something that should be consummated in the usual way, it should not be a relationship and he should not love me back. It was something that I had to do within myself.

I had to open up my heart, and when I looked at him, I could feel love, but then when this happened, I started to understand that it was not so easy just doing this because I actually had to go through this one and I had to feel it as if it were true.

Even if I knew that this was not a real love, I got sad. I got immensely sad about this love that could not, and should not, be fulfilled. It was a constant fight within me, but I was very determined to go this way where I could find out what this energy between him and me was about.

I had decided that I should open up my heart to him; that was a big part of my plan. And then in the midst of this… all this inner mess started to happen.

The first issue was that I became unhappily in love with him because I knew I was not supposed to be with him and I didn't want to, either. At the same time, I had to go through this feeling of not having the one I wanted. At the same time I felt this was something that was very important.

I didn't know why, but it was very important to learn that I should start loving people but not claim love in return. It was such a vague feeling, but it felt so important that I just knew I had to do it.

As I said, I started to withdraw from my life. Because something within me was in a constant feeling of despair which overwhelmed all the emotions that were going on.

It was a sea of waves moving around. I was crying, I was completely unhappy and I was so terrified of this because I felt a shift within me. Something was so different from what it used to be.

I started talking about love. What is love? What is it that everyone is talking about when they say that love is the foundation of the universe? It sounds so wonderful when everyone describes unconditional love and talks about staying with someone and being true. I was so curious about it. I wanted to learn it, I wanted to learn how to love unconditionally, but when I talked to people, I didn't get anywhere near an answer and it often seemed to me that people knew how to talk about it but were unable to practice it.

Another part of me changed too. I felt a sexual lust that was so overwhelming all the time. I had a constant desire for orgasms which slowly changed my life because it was always there. I was feeling as if I were just about to have an orgasm all the time, and I felt so embarrassed about it. I could not discuss it with anyone and it was tearing at my soul, emotions and body, this lust – as if a lot of small orgasms ran through my body when I was walking down the street, going to the supermarket or whatever I was doing.

And then this happened…

One day when I stayed in bed, my heart got in a cramp. The weird thing was that I wasn't scared that I was going to die; I knew that it had something to do with this energy. My body literally changed. I remember my heart going into cramps and at one point the cramp was so forceful that my heart stopped beating. My whole chest was changing, my heart was physically changing and I knew it was a big thing. It was as if something bigger was opening my heart, killing the old heart and replacing it.

After that, things got really weird and strange because something profound had happened within me, but I could not tell what it was.

Job application to god

I was in an emotional mess. And I felt so guilty because I believed I only had myself to blame. I felt I had brought myself to this because I had made a plan that was supposed to make me happy, but everything just got worse and I was very unhappy and frightened. This mess inside me and me trying to figure out my situation with my therapist eclipsed everything else in my life. I wanted it to change fast because I could see that my life was starting to fall apart.

When it happened, I felt I didn't need a therapist anymore – I needed a teacher, but I didn't know why and I didn't know what the difference was between having a therapist and having a teacher. I just knew that, in a very subtle way, there was a huge difference. That a teacher could guide me as a therapist couldn't.

I didn't know what to do. I was desperate for something to change because at this point, when I came to therapy, I didn't want it to be like this. It seemed to get worse for each time I was in the therapy room, and at the same time I didn't know where to go, so I had to stay.

I was also scared of leaving because if I left, I also left my inspiration. I was really worried about how do I find a teacher.

Then I got the idea of sending my therapist a job application. I was not sure that he was the one who was going to be my teacher, but I had nothing to lose by asking, and, as mentioned, I had no clue where else to go.

I sat down at my computer and wrote a job application.

I wrote:

"Dear God and the right man on earth, I would like to apply for this job that you have for me here on earth. I am an honest, hard-working, easy-learning woman, 33 years old and very eager to learn. I have always looked for something specific in my life, and I know I have found it and I want to learn it. I really hope that you would take me on board, and I will promise you that I will do anything to succeed. I am looking very much forward to hearing from you. Love, Lotte."

I sent him this by snail mail. I was so nervous the next time I came for a session. I was sitting there, and he looked at me, and he said, "You are very, very, very creative."

I said, "Yes, but do you want to be my teacher? I need something different."

He looked at me, and I was so terrified. Where do I go and what do I do if he says no. I could not bear it.

He said, "You are so creative. I can see what you want, but . . . "

This was the worst "but" in my whole life because I just knew the next thing that was coming was no.

He said no. I was completely devastated and I was in despair with myself and the whole situation. What should I do? I was in this mess and how could I get out of this mess?

If he was not saying "yes," what should I do?

I left that day, and my life was at its worst. It was dark. I was in turmoil. I was in a place I had never been before, and there were no people around me.

I had one more session with him, and when I went the next time, I was calmer because I thought that I had to let go now even though I was in such pain.

I sat down. I asked him not to sit in the chair opposite me. He had a sort of dining table in the same room, so we sat down there.

I looked at him, and I said, "I am going to leave today."

He looked at me as if to say, "This is not a good idea."

I said, "If you do not want me to learn this, there is nothing really that I can do."

He looked at me, and he said, "Well, I say yes, but then you will have to stand on your own."

It was a bit like saying yes to my job application, as if he said, *yes, and now I give you an assignment.*

That was all I needed because I knew exactly what he meant: "You need to stand on your own."

That day when I left the session room, I went out and it was as if, for the first time in my life, I needed to be in full charge of this situation. I have to do this. I have to stand on my own. I can't lean on him. I can't lean on anyone.

I have to learn this, and now I have a teacher.

Talking about an energy I see

When I talk about things I see, for instance an energy, I do not mean "see" in a physical way like seeing a door or a horse, but you probably know what I am talking about. I mean having these inner pictures which are very strong.

For me, they are real, and, sooner or later, they have all gained some meaning. Not that I always know what the meaning is when they appear to me, but they are my guidelines. What I started to see was the energy which I had been talking about for a while. I started seeing it, and it was taking shape; it was getting more and more physical for me.

When an energy first appears, it is very subtle and diffuse. In time, the energy starts to get more real. I start to see it, I feel it; it quite simply starts taking shape. I feel that it is there, but it is still very overwhelming because I can't really tell people about it in a way they understand, so it becomes a strange phenomenon which I have to explain in metaphors.

I was in a weird position because every time I talked, I felt that I sounded like a crazy person. I could see that part of myself out there, and see the expression in the faces of people who tried to understand me, and I could see they just thought I was crazy. I knew it was a delicate balance, but I was also convinced that I was not crazy and I knew that this was just a period in my life which I had to go through.

My aim was to learn about the energy, and I had to learn it fast because it was affecting my whole life on so many levels, and I felt so lost in my real life where I should just be and function.

These were also the talks I started having with my therapist/teacher because I was trying to learn what it was that I was seeing so he could guide me, but the talks turned out to be less helpful than I had hoped; he didn't know how to guide me. And deep within I knew I had to let go of him as a teacher almost from the very beginning because it was not right, but at the same time, I couldn't let go because then… I had no clue where to go.

Looking back

Looking back on this period of my life, I can see that something within me, in my soul, had been triggered, awakened, and it convinced that there was this greater thing for me. I got really hooked.

I also saw that when there is something deep inside which you want to manifest, you really have no choice. It is not possible to say no to this kind of challenge or experience in life. It happens and you must go with it. Even if I have regretted a million times that I ever did this in spite of it being so painful for myself and all the people around, it is hard to have regrets when you had no option. I realize now that it was impossible for me to do otherwise.

Having a fixed plan of what is a right life for me and how I should live it, or trying to control the outcome of my choices, has been hard for me and still is, and I guess it is a hard nut to crack for all human beings. I was quite simply fighting human nature.

It has been a huge lesson, living life according to a plan and trying to control that plan. I know that in a way it is a positive thing because it gave me direction and hope, but it also blocked the energy and made everything much worse than it had to be.

In India, for example, they have gurus, they have ashrams. They know what they are dealing with, and in that way they can guide people through those experiences. They have the knowledge and a calmer way of existing with it, but here in the west it is hard to find someone who can guide you. So I tried to make the therapist into something he was not, but the beauty of it was that I knew what I needed.

I have done so many good things for myself by following my nature. I can see now that all the knowledge I have later gained from books etc. , my inner guidance has already shown me, even with no one to teach me, and that makes me happy. That nature and I knew intuitively what to do, how to heal. A lot of people have said that you need a guru/teacher, and I also sensed that instinctively, but I also see that it was not my path. I have had many teachers in my everyday life, not one single person such as a guru to be in charge of my progress … and for me that's perfect, since I don't like to be dependent on anyone.

CHAPTER 3

The man and the woman

I see a picture of meaning

I was in this state now where my mind was constantly circling around this energy. I really wanted to capture it. I wanted to be able to express it verbally. I wanted to speak it.

I wanted to live this energy; it was so diffuse but so important. Every time I tried to tell myself that I didn't necessarily had to do it, I would feel really awful. I could feel it very clearly in my body and mind, but it was messy, it was a very strong hope and a very strong picture of where I could go. But how could I go there and how could I learn it? It was so difficult.

Suddenly the picture got clearer and I received this very strong picture of a man and a woman meeting in a special sacred union. I knew that if they came from a state of consciousness, they could merge completely. It was like one person became light and the other person would become light, and then they would become fully light together and in a way disappear together... I got so excited... I know this was what I wanted to create in real life.

I wanted to be that woman who could do that with a man, and I wanted to meet that man whom I could do that with. This part turned out to be the greatest pain because I knew deep within that it was also a reflection of my inner man and my inner woman. Even if my body really wanted a man to show me this, I also knew that basically it was a picture of me obtaining that wisdom of being a woman in that state of consciousness who could attract the same state in others. I knew that I was able to get there, but the stress I put on myself in doing too fast made everything much worse.

I was really stuck, and at the same time I was not stuck, because I knew where I wanted to go, what I wanted to learn... I just didn't know how to gain it because I knew this was a healing. I knew that when I arrived I would be able heal the wound in myself.

The union is the healing – I see it, but how?

As I said, this picture became my life saviour in a way because I had this picture within me of where I could go, what the goal was, what kind of state of consciousness I could be in, and this was the lesson that I was going for in healing; this spontaneous kundalini.

At that point, I didn't know it was kundalini from a conscious state, but because I had this picture, I knew I would not lose my touch with reality because this was greater than becoming crazy.

This picture became my guidance, but it is so hard to have this inner picture and at the same time still need help. Especially when those you ask for help do not understand it.

I had my therapist, and I was trying desperately to talk to him about this. Because he was also the inspiration of this meeting, I was stuck because I felt that, in a way, I was projecting all this on him, but, at the same time, I wanted to take responsibility for being my inner healing.

It was very difficult for me to accept that I had not arrived yet but still had a long way to go. It was so frustrating that I could not verbalize my goal, but my belief in the goal helped me and made me go through this journey without losing my mind.

A trip to the forest – nature

While I was writing, my sexual energy was very present all the time. I was so happy to have just the occasional minute when I was not thinking about sex, not feeling lust in my body, feeling an energy as if a man were entering me all the time.

I felt as though I was walking through life and making love at the same time, and I was extremely embarrassed about it because I thought that if people could see how I felt, and how could they just want to talk with me while all this lust was going on inside me? I could not find a way to be at ease with it because it was constantly tearing through my body, and it could come in the weirdest places all the time.

Masturbation became a means of survival, too. When I did it, for a moment I could be in a space where nothing was going on, the energy would stop causing havoc in my body and I was relieved for a short period of time.

I started getting addicted to having these orgasms because they gave me that space of peace where there was no warm energy burning in my body; it gave me a short reprieve from constantly thinking about this energy or constantly focusing on sex and lust which felt as if someone was taking over my soul and my body. It was this huge energy taking control of my body.

It was like someone giving you a rocket instead of a car. When you turn on the engine, you thought it was a car, but it was not a car, it was a rocket. That was the feeling I had in my body all the time.

I didn't understand the aggression of this sexuality. It wasn't nice. It was violating and it felt as if it had more power than I had. In a way, I was obsessed with this sexual energy, but I also felt as if I was possessed by an energy. What to do with it? What could I do with all this energy?

Then I had an idea, and I have been very happy that I really listened to what my body needed: I started taking walks in the forest. I had never done that before.

I drove up north to a special forest every time. I felt like a child in a candy store when I walked into the forest. Often I took up a handful of soil and smelled it, and it calmed down my system.

I walked into a place far away from where other people would come. I could play around, so I jumped onto the fallen tree trunks, I played with the leaves, I jumped about among the trees. I felt so connected with Mother Earth when I was there.

What I realized was that it felt as if I got so connected with Mother Earth that all the sexual energy became much more sensual when I was there, as if Mother Nature was making love with me, and we became one. I felt supported by her and all this energy.

I want to explain

I was in such a desperate situation when I tried to explain this to the therapist. I really wanted him to understand what it was that I wanted to learn. I had this idea that if I could really make him understand what I needed to learn, he could teach me - at least that was my logical thought.

My approach was too logical, as it turned out. As if you can take something like universal love and put it into a box, and then learn this box. Nevertheless, such was my plan. I was scared that if I didn't have a plan, everything would just fall completely apart, so I had this very rigid notion that I just needed to learn this, and that notion wasn't helpful at all.

For how do you learn universal love? After all, there is no teacher you can look up in the phone book. You won't find a search criteria such as, *"I want to learn about universal love and I want to learn how to have that in my body so I can be this in my life."*

I started getting really angry with my therapist because I couldn't understand all these nice words, all this oneness, all this fantastic energy and so on – but it felt like an illusion and I was terrified, but still I felt I had no choice, and that pissed me off too.

The drawing

One day I was going to a therapy session. I was sitting in a café, and I felt as if volumes of ancient knowledge passed through me. So I went to the stationery shop, and I bought a notebook that had this "very old book" design; the paper was yellow and wrinkled and I chose this 19th-century style because I wanted to convey the impression that I did not really wish to explain myself to my therapist but something much greater, and I wanted the style of the notebook to reflect that.

I sat down, and I thought, "I am going to draw this to him. I can't explain it and I can't find the words, but I can draw it." So I did that. I saw an "X" and a "Y" and it was about the merging of the man and the woman, and you could see that in the fact box underneath the drawing what it was what I was trying to explain to him.

When I saw that, things became much easier. I thought that now he would understand, because he would now be able to see it, and it isn't about him and me but about something universal, and because I can draw it he can see that this is something that is actually real.

Looking back right now as I am writing this, I can see I was being quite naïve, but that was the thought I had and life is a step-by-step learning all the time, I guess. You see the waves in the drawing, and in the drawing, one line is a man and the other one is a woman.

If she is clean and he is clean in his waves, they are light. There are no filters on it. They are just clean. When they meet in the energy points (you can see that in the middle), they can merge completely.

When they merge completely, they still feel like separate entities, they still feel like individuals, but they also feel united into one. So the two become one, and the one becomes two.

I thought it was beautiful, and I thought "this is the way I want to be." I thought, "Now I have this drawing. I am going to go down and show him that now I found the key. Now, he will understand," and I had so much joy in my heart when I took my bicycle and while I was cycling through town.

It was cold, and it was dark, but it was such a joy. I had this old book and I had this great drawing, and I felt now there is hope, now we can start working because I didn't really feel I was going anywhere before that.

Now I felt I was beginning, and that we could start working.

I understand subconsciously what it was which I was in the middle of when I saw the drawing

I came to his consultation room, and I was very joyful inside. I was very hopeful. I was very excited to show him the drawing. I went inside. I was a bit nervous.

He looked at me and said, "Hi!"

I said, "Hi!"

He said, "How are you doing?"

I said I was doing fine, and I said, "I have something to show you." I took out my drawing and I thought that he was going to be really excited about it. That he was going to think it would be the most amazing thing he had ever seen.

I said, "I have drawn it. Now I know what it is. I can show you."

He said, "Let me see it."

I showed it to him. He looked at it, and then he said, "That is a nice drawing."

I thought, "What? A nice drawing? Is that all you can say?" I didn't say that out loud, but I was thinking it when he said, "a nice drawing." When he said that, I understood that we were so many miles apart that he could not teach me this.

It freaked me out! I was sitting there and I was looking at this drawing, and I could see that he was so not in tune with it... at all! This was not his way. It was so hard for me to accept that he was not willing or wanting to go this way with me.

I was blank. I could see his eyes were still looking at this drawing and he was looking at me. Then I looked at the drawing, and some place inside me woke up and I saw what I had drawn.

It was not just a man and a woman, and I could not quite grasp it in a conscious way, but something inside me knew it, and he didn't say it out loud, but there was this feeling that was like "I'm not going to touch this," and that was the first time I really felt like no one wants to help healing this... this kundalini stuff.

When I was looking at it, I understood subconsciously that this was something going on in me – this energy was me. When I looked at it, I could see that it was something that I had seen before, that wavy kind of style that you see when someone is drawing a kundalini.

I felt like this was the healing, and it was something that I had put outside me, but I didn't want to learn about the kundalini, I wanted to learn about the man and the woman because I felt that that was the healing part for me in the state I was in.

That drawing changed a lot of things.

I lost my teacher

After this meeting, I was completely blank. I didn't know what to do now. What happened at this time, too, was that the therapist education I had been attending stopped. I stopped because I was not in a state where I could become a therapist.

That also meant that I lost touch with the teacher who had been there for a long time in my life, I lost that connection and the whole network of all my students around me which provided some sort of buffer for me. I lost that, and the therapist. After that meeting with the drawing, we went for a walk, and he was not there anymore. I lost him.

Within a very short time, I lost all the people around me that I felt a connection with and from whom I could get some help in all this. I felt extremely lost and I was terrified. I couldn't give up, and I didn't want to, either. It was as if I didn't have any words, because at that time I thought that if you have pain in your heart or you have anxieties, you can go to a therapist, and I could not go to therapy anymore. If I could not go to therapy, where, then, could I go?

I just wished I had this very old person, someone wise around me who could tell me something, show me something – but there was none. There was just me, with all this extremely raw energy.

I felt so alone and so lost. Normally, I would read books about subjects, but I was too scared to read because I felt that if I was reading anything about it, it would just turn on the energy even more.

I started drawing this energy a lot, and I was trying in many ways to explain life through this drawing – what it was all about.

One day, I hung up all of these drawings on the walls. They were all there, and then the energy started to open up so much space, and I just felt as if I got so much greater knowledge about the whole structure of the human being. I could see how souls were composed of different energy strings, patterns, but I had no idea what it was. It was so overwhelming, and I got so scared. Then when I felt most open, a picture of a woman came and she said "come"... I looked at her and at that moment I knew that I would have to say the strongest "no" in my life, because I felt she was inviting me into insanity...

Anxiety

The anxiety started to become so intense, and it was constantly present. Before then, I had been curious for a long time and I just opened up to see it. I had seen the pictures, I had seen all the energies, I had felt all the sensations, and then suddenly, with this immense anxiety, the energy was so overwhelming that it was as if I had opened up fully. As if I had endless doors open. I had them open all at the same time in this determination to get to the truth so I could start living again.

For a long time, I had opened up, I had talked, I had been curious. Even though I had been scared and overwhelmed, I had tried repeatedly to open up and talk and talk and see and understand.

Suddenly I was in this fully open space, and I felt as if it had all opened far too much, and it was not good. It was so bad that I could not do anything. The energy had taken over my whole life, and I was stuck.

I am a problem solver. I had this problem, and normally I would just phone someone and say, "I have this and that problem, will you help me solve it?" That is my style, but I could not call anyone. I was stuck. I was lost.

My mind was in pain, my body too, and my soul, and I was so sad – very sad that I had done this to myself. I thought I could open up for it and understand it quite quickly, and then just move on.

I started realizing that I had done something to myself which was very hurtful for me and for everything in my life.

Looking back

When I look back on this period of my life, I can see that something deep within was healing me in a way, and that I really wanted to find all the good solutions. I wanted to have a teacher. My body went to nature. It was looking for something that could nurture me.

I see with tremendous gratitude that something very deep within really tried to help me and knew which things were right to do. My body was showing me the way all the time, which saved me many times, and I knew when it was time to leave things. I left my education, I left the therapist even if I didn't want to. Maybe I didn't really leave him, but hanging around was no option.

It was a lesson in starting to learn to see what was the truth in me, meeting the reality I was in, and seeing what was out there for me. This was the beginning of this huge lesson of seeing what is actually real all the time. What is the truth right here? What is good for me?

Looking back, I also see how scared I was. I was really scared and love didn't help, because I felt that if I loved people, they misunderstood me.

I also see that just talking about love is not enough. We always talk about love, living from the heart, especially in all these workshops I have been in. We talk about oneness – we talk and talk, but we are in fact scared of showing love to each other.

It was that state of mind, heartfulness, which I wanted to learn. I am very grateful that I had that greater picture of where I could go and I could really feel how it was inside me when I had obtained it.

I could feel that sensation in my body even though I was not there yet. It was a life saver for me; it meant that I constantly believed because I could feel that greater space for me, I also knew I could go there.

I also knew every time it didn't match the feeling outside, I was not there yet. Right at that point, I was very hard on myself because I wanted to be there NOW. It could not go fast enough, but it was a very important part of the process.

Looking back, I also learned something about these orgasms. I read about kundalini afterwards. I read that some teachers tell you not to masturbate, that the energy just has to run through nicely, but it didn't.

I can see that because the energy kundalini's direction is to run out through the spine, up in the neck and up in the brain and then receive, and be with, this greater consciousness, it takes you where you see a much bigger picture of the world - but when the brain is not ready, we can go crazy with this energy.

If it goes up in the brain and you are not consciously prepared for it, you can really make a mess of your brain.

CHAPTER 4

Awakening

Full-blown awakening

The meltdown came suddenly. I started feeling really bad. It was not just anxiety anymore, and it was not just frustration about it and how to solve it. My body showed me that something was really wrong.

I started to be unable to orientate myself. For example, there was one day I went into a park. I have a very good sense of direction, but when I went into this park, I could not get out. I was trapped in a labyrinth and every time I walked in one direction, I got lost again.

It was a very simple park with many exits. It freaked me out. It was not just anxiety where you feel scared and you feel this is overwhelming, but it started to show me that something was really bad and I was losing that overview. I had felt for a long time I had something to say, but right now I felt I had nothing to say.

I also drove around in a car one day, and I knew my goal but I had no idea how to get there. At that time, I was going to Clay Cookie that evening. I ended up at many other places, but I could not find the way to that specific place.

When I finally got there, I just sat down and my teacher sensed that I was not in a very calm state. I just took the clay, and that night I made seven sculptures in two hours.

I did a lot of sculptures in which you could see the whole spine. I did the male and the female spine and so many variations of it. I had to cool off somehow so I just felt like sitting there, and the teacher just let me sit there. I felt peaceful.

I went to the hospital one day because everything was a mess. They thought I had a brain tumor because all my symptoms indicated that something was going on in my brain. I went to scanning, but it came out negative. I was in shock because my whole system was literally closing down.

When I came back from the scanning at the hospital, I went to my own doctor. She started asking questions. I could just sense that if I said "yes" in the wrong place and "no" in the wrong place, she might put me on medication, and I could tell by her look that she was thinking, *What is her mental state?*

I knew that if I had been truthful that day, she would have sent me to a psychiatrist, and I didn't want to go there because I knew that might make me even worse.

The only thing I really wanted was for her to tell me I was sick so I could take time off from work and have some peace, and she did that although I could also see in her face that she was not really okay with it. She was not sure if that was enough.

She gave me a note so I could be home on sick leave and get some rest. I knew that the doctor was not the right person to see, and I was still in this space where could I heal this, now that everything was burned down. I had to do something because I was really ill now. I was no longer able to work.

I took time off, and I thought I had hit rock bottom.

Then when I think it can't get any worse

I was going to Majorca. It was nice just to be with family and just in a state where I could be calm and relaxed. I thought maybe I could get my health back now, and that the energy would subside.

One night I woke up because it started to burn so much in my lower back. It was as if I was on fire. I had felt this burning before, but this time it was much more intense. I sat there in the dark and I started drawing my pain because I had to do something. Suddenly, I saw this huge crystal going from my spine up to the top, and I saw a snake rising up, and I became that snake.

When it happened, I knew this was getting really serious. I had indeed hit rock bottom. Now it was here. Now it was real. I thought I was going crazy, that I was losing it, and I felt that everything was dissolving around me.

I had tried to do everything in my life to prevent this from happening. That was why I was in such a hurry to try to find the result and solution for all this, I thought, because I had subconsciously known that this would come.

It had been two years, and now it was there. I couldn't *not* face it anymore. I was terrified because I felt it was not real. I felt I was going mad. It was so hard staying present and feeling grounded in my body and just stay there. I felt I was flying away.

There was an immense irony about being in Alcudia, Majorca with all these tourist places when I had this awakening, this full-blown awakening.

In some way, because I was in this place, it forced me to be real and stay real and be present in life because I had no choice. I was surrounded by so many people I knew and I had to avoid going crazy. That was my luck, being in Alcudia, Majorca, when my now full-blown kundalini occurred.

The call to my therapist

I woke up the next day, and I was so scared.

I called my therapist. We had not talked for quite a while. I said to him that I was in Majorca and told him what had happened the night before. "I am burning wildly now and I feel I am losing it. They thought I had a brain tumor. I feel lost. I have this crystal in my spine, I see a snake," and I asked, "Is this what I think it is? Is this a kundalini?"

He said yes, and he also told me that he had seen it coming. He said to me, "This is not something you can choose to go through; this is something you *have* to go through."

I have often thought about that statement because I felt I no longer had a choice; I really had to go with it now. He also said, "Don't drink. Exercise."

For me, it was not so much what it was specifically, I focused on living very healthily now, really taking care of myself.

I could also sense that he was not there to support me in this. He was not telling me to come up and let him see how things were. He was more like *I have to go*.

I just sat there, and this was the wildest thing. There was really no one around in my life to understand and support what I was going through.

When I hung up, I put my on running shoes. I went down to the beach. I actually think I took off my shoes and just ran in the water and in the sand with my bare feet. I felt I had to stay grounded, I felt that I had to stay 100% true to everything in my life or I would lose it altogether.

It was a warm day, and I could hear all the screaming kids from where they were bathing and people laughing and people talking, but it was a bit like a tape, as if I were not really there.

But I had no choice. It was my journey. Right now, I was completely alone, and I had to get well.

I got rid of everything that is not needed

Since I didn't know what to do, I went back to my core and myself. That was the only thing I could do.

I scraped off everything that was not needed in my life – relationships, friends. Everything I my life was at a total minimum.

I felt as if I had just been born again, and that I had to learn everything from scratch. I had to respect the energy now that it ran amuck in my body, and I had to respect it because I could not make it go away. I wanted it to go away, but I had to cope with it in some way which I believed would be helpful. I had to listen hard every second, every day.

Life became very, very slow. It was about being fully present in everything. I ate when I really felt I had to eat, which was a little bit throughout the day. I could not put anything in my body that my body didn't want to eat. It could be a very specific thing I wanted to eat one day, and another thing the next day. When I was walking in the street, I might have had an idea that I wanted to do a specific thing, and I wanted to go there, but my body just could not. Many times I wanted to go left but my body wanted to go right, and I felt I had to listen.

Every time I didn't listen to my body, the energy just revolted in my body and I got dizzy and I got anxious and I felt like I was just empty space. Every time I listened, it calmed down. This became a barometer for doing what was right for me.

I had no choice because I knew I would lose myself if I did not obey. It was like taking baby steps all the time – asking, "is this good? No. Yes." At that time, life became very tight and became very "just me" and what was necessary for me to make every day pass.

Slowly, it felt as if, all over again, I had to learn to walk. I had to move rather than being completely frozen.

I was also very lucky at that time that my job was in a kindergarten/nursery for children from one to three years old. I went to work every day. Routines there were at a very slow pace. I practiced being present with the kids all the time. That way, they were healing me because you had to do things slowly – you taught them things slowly, you walked slowly, we ate slowly, we painted slowly.

This was basically what I needed, too. When we were in the playground, we could play in the sand and it could be really fascinating just to let the sand run through my fingers. I was really aware of this extremely slow pace, so for me watching the sand going through my fingers was just as exciting as it was for them because I was practicing being present more than ever in my life, being me with my body and my soul and my mind, together with those children. They taught me that.

I feel very grateful that they were in my life just at the right time. You can say that I didn't have an old wise man or woman around to guide me, but I had all these kids and right there I learned that anything in life can be your teacher. Because I didn't have anyone else, everything in life became my teacher together with my awareness.

Walk and talk therapy

When I started getting to a point when I felt I was feeling a bit more together, I remembered a therapist whom I know vaguely. I knew she was very grounded. I called her and went to some of her sessions.

In the beginning, she did some therapy and I was very scared that she would go the same way as many other therapists would have gone. Since I felt that I had this monster living inside me, I didn't want to talk about it, not directly. I feared that talking about it or thinking about it too much would mess it up even more.

I was so scared of telling anyone what had happened, because I felt it was all my own fault. Even worse, I had planned to fall in love with a man and then I had difficulty falling out of love, and I didn't even want him.

I was in this anxiety mode of being afraid that the energy would take over and would put me in a non-stop panic attack mode.

When I exercised discipline, such as eating the right things, drinking no alcohol and having walks only where my body wanted to walk, only seeing the people I wanted to see – I felt as if I could just be, without feeling that I was losing it completely.

I went to the therapist. In the beginning, we were sitting there in front of each other like traditional therapists and clients do. I had done heaps of therapy at that time, so I knew all the tricks and I knew what she was doing. Every time something felt too therapeutic, I got completely locked up.

One day she was asking a therapeutic question and I was trying to answer it, but I just couldn't do therapy, so I left the room.

She came out, and she said, "Look at me," and I said, "Don't take me apart. I am one. I am whole." I just had to believe that so immensely at that point, that I was one whole part and I could go through this. If she was breaking me up in therapeutic pieces, I was afraid I would fall apart.

Then she did something. She looked at me and said, "That's completely fine. Do you want to go for a walk?"

I said "Yes!"

So we left the room. There was a lake in the city and we took a walk around it. For the first time in a long while, I felt that someone was just being a human being with me without me having to change anything, without having to analyze anything. We just walked, and we talked about life in general.

When I came back to her therapy room, I do not think I even went in. We just said good-bye, and I said, "Thank you so much! Can we do this again?" and she said, "Of course."

For a long time, I started going to her, and we went for walks through the city, and just talked. This was my walk-and-talk therapy. The fantastic thing was that I only needed to talk a little bit about my problem, and she knew what was happening. She was the first one who started to know a little bit about it.

We didn't analyze it, and we didn't have to do anything about it. She just knew that I was in this special space. Once in a while, when it was too cold outside or the weather was bad, we lay down on some mattresses. She had a big room next to her therapy room in that apartment, and we just had tea and talked.

Although she was a therapist, she didn't do therapy. She was just being a fellow human with me. At the same time, she was also very professional. It was great to have one person in your life who was simply there – who could just be there. That was all I really needed, and it slowly calmed down my system.

Looking back

Looking back now at this period of my life, I have the greatest respect for my body because, as I learned later on, my body followed its nature. I have heard it is good to eat a little bit all the time, for instance, feeding the energy so it does not go over-hungry and run wild.

I also got a tip that milk was good for me. I heard that later on. I didn't drink milk, though, but I ate a lot of cheese back then. I ate healthy food. I exercised. Yoga, for example, was good for me. I did some other exercises, and I walked a lot so I got grounded.

I did things slowly, so I got even more grounded. I have this incredible gratitude towards my body and my ears, especially my ears because I listened – listened to my body.

Also, I know that there are so many opinions about this kundalini rising and a lot of people strive to get that awakening.

The irony is I got something that other people spend years yearning for, and I didn't even want it. I think that has been something that had cost me even more pain with it; I was fighting it because I didn't want it.

There is no right way in kundalini. You can get guidance on how to do it and get through it in the best way, and there are some ground rules that probably work. Then, again, some rules work for some people and some rules do not.

The kundalini is a reflection of a human being who is going through that specific awakening and that is why there will be different ways to heal it because the symptoms and reactions, you might say, are very different from each person – also, it differs how much cleansing needs to be done.

Looking back, I am so grateful for my stubbornness – I am very stubborn. I didn't want to be mentally sick. I could see no point in sitting in a mental institution. It was just not an option for me.

That has been my survival. That there was no option. It was not a solution I wanted; therefore, we were not going that way, no matter how hard it was, no matter how lost I felt, it was not a solution. I wanted to have a fantastic life, and I wanted it to be good, and I wanted to be healthy.

I was, in a way, extremely optimistic in all this mess and in all this pain. There is always a doorway out of any mess. This is the belief that drives me onwards: that there is always something that can lead me somewhere. There is always a door. You just have to find it.

Sometimes I get lost, and sometimes I find the wrong door or I have to open ten doors that were not the right ones, but they taught me a little bit, and then I found the door that I felt was better for me.

Also looking back, all this obsession with being a clean human being suddenly profited me because if I had not cleansed as much as I have done if the energy had not intervened. I probably would have been much worse off, but I made a habit of cleansing, and I knew I had to do it whenever kundalini was kicking in.

That is the way it is today. I have to become more aware every time when kunda kicks in because she is telling me something. I get kundalini sick as I call it, because I have stayed in bed so often for days, because I felt such turmoil in my body. When I get an awareness of what I need to change in life, then the energy calms down. It has been nonstop work… to become more aware and clean.

The more I cleansed and became aware, the closer I got to my truth and to getting better.

CHAPTER 5
Shutting down

For a while, I was much better

After some time living as who I really was, things were okay, and I managed. I was moving forward slowly, and it felt as if I was getting back to a state where I was no longer on constant alert.

I felt I had shut everything out of my life which didn't help me anymore.

I went to see a healer. I can't quite understand why, but I wanted some confirmation that this was actually what had happened. I needed someone to tell me that I am not crazy, that this is real, and that this stuff is actually happening. I got the healer's name from the therapist I had seen before.

I told him about my situation, and he confirmed that this energy was indeed a kundalini, and I felt that to be a comfort. He also said he could see that I had been just on the point of losing my mind. I do not know why, but it was nice that some person recognized that I had been so far out and also that I had been able to walk back off the plank and not losing it.

He then wanted to heal me, but I didn't want that. Even if he had been completely clean, I was so scared that just a slight drop of dirty energy would disrupt everything again.

He looked at me and thought I was a bit off kilter since I didn't want help in that way, but I had what I wanted, and it was a recognition of what had happened. Then he said that I should walk in nature. I told him that I had done that for a long time, but I listened to him. I continued walking in parks and nature and on beaches and in forests – any place where I connected to nature.

Again, I was happy that I had actually heard this command within myself; that my body had guided me to nature without anyone telling me.

My body wanted to heal naturally. I walked and walked and walked – a good walk to the beach and just going for a long, long walk. Receiving that energy from Mother Earth which was very much the one I was connecting to.

Also in this period, and because I had shut everything out of my life, I understood how lonely this journey was, and that I was all by myself. In a way, I know that we are all connected, but I also know we are very much alone. When something like this happens, you are extremely alone.

I felt as though the kundalini had become my education, my job as the seeker to unwrap all the lies within me so I could hear my own voice and more clearly be myself. Therefore, it was impossible for me to be around lies from other people, but it also became very hard to be with my own lies, for at that time there were still many. Today, there are still places where I do not want to face the truth, and I am happy for that because it means I am only human.

But in all this, I felt loneliness. I felt lonelier than ever. I also felt strong because I had come so far and actually managed to avoid going crazy; I had a certain amount of will power and I was grateful for it.

At the same time, I thought I could close a chapter back then, even if I was in control of what was going on. I was not relaxed with it, but I had hoped that I could close this chapter in my life now that I had come this far, and yet I had no clue at that time how far I still had to go in order to get much nearer to what I had set out to accomplish.

I shut down the energy

At this time, three years had gone since I had started my journey, and I felt I was in a state where I was sort of okay. I was not in tip-top condition, but I no longer felt I was going crazy.

At this point, I had not slept for almost two years because the energy had been pumping around inside. I was constantly half tired, and it ended up being like that for 10 years.

Then what happened in my life was that something needed my attention 100%.
I felt the outer life suddenly yelling at me, and I made a decision to pack up all this kundalini. I took all my drawings and everything and wrapped it up, trusting that this would never be needed again in my life.

I feel I messed up that inner voice that had promised me a fantastic life. I felt I messed it up really bad, and I was actually going almost crazy. I did not want therapy, I did not want to do anything. This is a chapter that has been and now it is done.
There was still a lot of unresolved energy in my soul. The picture I had seen of the man and the woman, I was nowhere near that, but I just could not go further, so I shut it down. I shut down my soul's voice.
I felt like I could live now, and I could cope with what was needed in the outside world, and that was very important for me at that time. It was also very hard to shut down that inner voice, but there was something much greater for me right now, I felt.

It is impossible

I thought this decision about shutting the energy down was really good. I truly believed at that point that I could do it, that I could actually shut down that energy forever and ever and just stay like that.
What happened then was that I started to get really bitter because I had

shut out the possibility of realizing my dream about a fantastic life and going to the deep place that had been calling for me all my life. I had no clue at that point how much it affected me, but it was like shutting down my soul.

What I saw was that I started getting really angry; I was getting bitter, I was yelling at everything and everyone, and I felt trapped. I felt punished by the bigger picture. I felt punished by God.

I felt punished for wanting something which I believed at that point to be unobtainable. I felt punished for trying to believe in something that was so much bigger than me; something that was not very easy to grasp, but still, I knew it was there. I felt I was punished for wanting that, for wanting something that was so great for my soul.

I felt that I had betrayed everyone around me if I wanted that, that I was not a good person. There was this battle within me which felt like *either/or*. If I was going for my soul, I felt that I was not doing my best for everyone else in my life. For that, I punished myself even more.

The anger and the bitterness were starting to take up a lot of space in my life, and it was starting to poison everyone around me. My soul just wanted something else. It could not just stay in this situation.

I wish it had not been like that. I think that is why I got trapped. When we listen to our souls, we can't plan it so it goes the way we think would be the best way. That has been the hardest part for me to accept - that I could not get it the way I wanted it.

I felt punished by the greater picture, and I also punished myself for not being as good as I might be.

What do I do and where do I go?

I guess I was coming to the conclusion that I just didn't want to be bitter and angry for the rest of my life. I was much too young to be a grumpy old woman, and it was not really the person I am, nor was it funny to see myself being so unhappy.

CHAPTER 5 • SHUTTING DOWN

The question came again, "where do I go and what should I do?" I felt that the drawing was one way to begin; that meeting with the female and the male. I could start writing about it and try once again to discover what this energy was, and then see if I could put it into words so I could understand it. That was my new plan. And yet again... the plans... they don't work.

I felt that if I could write it, I could see my voice, I could hear my voice, I could understand what I wanted to tell myself and learn, and then subsequently act on it.

I decided I wanted to write this book about the male and the female and the energy and the drawings. Again, I just needed someone to guide me. In a way, I probably wanted what I wanted before, the teacher – but no one was around.

I contacted my first therapist where it had all had started because I felt I should go back to the source again, the inspiration.

I called the therapist, and he said yes, he would do that.

I thought it might lead me somewhere, it might help me, but the energy was simply not there and he didn't know how to guide me. I was stuck in this situation again where I could not get it out on my own and I was too dependent on someone else, and I really didn't know what to do.

The pain and the anger and the bitterness and the mess took another rollercoaster ride. I so badly missed someone who could guide me – just guide me a little bit - but it didn't happen.

I stopped trying to write with him. It faded out. There was simply no creative energy here, and I got stuck.

I had tried to shut it down, and now I tried to open, but that didn't work either, and I could not shut it down – such makes me sick and it makes my soul sick, and I didn't want to do that for the rest of my life.

I was constantly on the lookout for people who could help me. I sometimes googled for people who knew about energy, who could help me make the drawing about energy ... but what is that? I didn't want to go to therapy anymore. I didn't like those vibes, they were too heavy. I needed someone to teach me.

It was the same thing – the same story over and over again. I felt so stuck. There is no such helper to be found around the corner of a 7/11, and no one to be found in the phone book. I was screaming inside, *where are the right people?*

This was my solution: Get rid of the kundalini, I want my life, period!

Looking back

Looking back, I can see at this point how much I thought that kundalini didn't fit into my life and also, the weirdest thing, actually because the kundalini *is* me. It was as if I didn't fit into my own life. I didn't fit me.

I wanted life to be in a specific way, and I think a lot of people get stuck in what they imagine does not match what they want. Then, at the same time, maybe this is the key to all happiness, just choosing to be ourselves all the time.

I can see how much I have hurt myself by wanting to get rid of the energy because in fact I wanted to get rid of myself and the way I was. I felt I always made the wrong choices by being me.

I could not understand why so many people wanted this kundalini thing. I didn't understand the urge to sit down for hours in the hope of receiving this energy. It was such a big puzzle to me. Why is this cool? I asked myself. Why do people do this?

I never wanted it, and I felt it was ruining my life. It just filled me up with pain and unhappiness and sorrow.

I can also see, in retrospect, that I tried to shut down my soul's inner voice. Now I know that this is impossible.

That voice is what we are really here for. We are here to listen to that voice and obey it. I believe a lot of the illness and anger and bitterness we see in the world exists because we do not live as we are intended to live – live as the ones we are – so we turn it into a battle. I know I did. I battled with myself and I battled with the very deep core of my soul. Such battles will never have a happy outcome.

CHAPTER 6

The helping people arrive

Body talk[1]

Over time, when I met someone who was a therapist or anyone in that area, I started vaguely talking about kundalini. Some didn't know what it was, but some accepted it. I started to open a little door to connect with the outer world.

I met those two roads – the ones that said *it is a blissful thing, mine was really nice*, and then I met those who said *this is hell, you should get out of it.* What could I say? I agreed with the last one.

Through some connections I had, I met a health care system called BodyTalk. At that point, I had dropped everything that was therapy, basically anything that could help me. I was so scared that the energy would blow off if anyone treated me.

Then I met BodyTalk, and it became a huge turnaround in my life which I had no idea about the first time. I had my first BodyTalk session with a woman. I told her I was really scared. I have this thing, what can I do? I was scared that it would trigger it off again because I was still in this very controlled place and worried about letting others into my energy.

She said that BodyTalk could do no harm. The body is just going to balance exactly what it can, and it will never do more than it can take in that moment.

I felt a bit safe by that, and I felt the energy was very kind. I needed

---

1. Read more at about the system here at www.bodytalksystem.com.
© IBA International BodyTalk Association.

kindness for my healing. I laid down, and I had my first BodyTalk session. When I had that one, I felt safe for the first time in many years. I felt I was in a place where some healing could start and it would not do any harm.

It was amazing. It was amazing to talk about the energy a little and then have the sessions afterwards. I felt as if a new door had opened, and I found something that could really heal me, so I opened that door much more.

I opened up the door to BodyTalk much more, and I started learning the system of this fantastic healing system that I had come across. It was amazing to get these sessions and see that it made my system relax. I could suddenly see how controlled I was in holding the kundalini.

BodyTalk is taught all over the world. A completely new chapter started in my life because for me, going to BodyTalk seminars around the world was not just going to a seminar to learn some knowledge but the travel itself made the healing.

Every time I sat down, I booked a seminar somewhere in the world to learn more about BodyTalk. I knew something new was going to transform, not just the learning process but the whole thing about going to a seminar.

I now felt for the first time I was on the right track. I felt that finally something was going to change, big time. I never had that feeling before when all this had happened. It had always been like *where are they? I feel alone. I am lost!* Suddenly, just the feeling of having it in my life was amazing.

The first seminar I took was in England, learning the system. I felt that I was with people who had this kindness towards the human being. It was not about pushing anything because BodyTalk is never about pushing anything. The body is actually telling exactly what it needs to heal right now.

After I had been to my first seminar in England, I quickly booked my next seminar in Northern Ireland. I remember I sat down, and in these two days I learned all this material about consciousness and I understood that the healing was the place I was in, the teacher who was there, the participants who were there.

When I left that seminar, I started meeting teachers who understood what it was I was in. They didn't point fingers. They didn't say it was scary, didn't say it was easy. They didn't say anything. They just knew that I was going through some major shift and I was in this natural state for this to happen. That in itself was so amazing.

The other thing that was amazing was that they were talking about energy, consciousness – that consciousness *is* energy. I felt that suddenly, all that I had in my mind was starting to unfold itself in front of my eyes. People were talking about this crazy and weird stuff I had been through, they were just talking about it.

I thought, "wow, all these people around the world are talking about this, and that is just amazing."

My first meeting with Italy

I had signed up for a seminar in Italy, and I had booked my flight and now I was ready to go. It seemed like the ones I had attended when I met my first therapist and was looking at all the seminars that were going on, and I just saw this one that I had to go to.

It was in Italy, and I just had to go. It was beaming out at me. I booked my ticket, and some days before I had an email from the head office that there was an extra day to the seminar if I was interested. It was a day before the actual dates, and I thought I wanted to do that, that I wanted to go, so I bought a new ticket.

I went to the airport. I was so excited. I felt that this was going to be fantastic. I am going to Italy, not that far from Venice. When I went to the airport, I saw that I had bought the wrong ticket. It was for another day.

I was standing in the airport. I wanted to go because the extra day was the following day; I had two flight tickets and could not use them, so within five minutes I had to buy a third flight ticket just to go.

I could feel that this was so important to go to that I had no second thoughts. I just had to go, but it is a bit funny to think that I ended up buying three tickets to go to a seminar, but who cares... it was a very important seminar.

When I arrived in Italy, it was amazing. I had not been to Italy for many, many years. I had only been there once in my teenage years; I had been on interrail trains and it had not been such a happy trip, so I didn't have any great expectations concerning Italy, but I was completely amazed when I landed there.

It was as if I woke up. Wow, Italy! What is it? There was something inside me that fit so well, like a puzzle finally starting to come together. Like all these pieces had been spread out when kundalini entered my life. Suddenly, breaks were coming into my life that might make me whole again.

Just being in Italy started healing me. I do not know in what way, but I started laughing. I ate fantastic food. The people who were at the seminar were like family I had been reunited with. It was the language, it was the food, it was the energy. It was everything.

It was so yummy for my soul. I felt I was swimming in joyful energy in everyone. The talks I had. I met people with whom I could talk about the kundalini.

It was so amazing that I could sit at a dinner table and I could talk about this kundalini, and people would say *yes, I completely understand.*

I had not had that feeling for a long time. It felt that they were supporting my soul's journey. I felt something very Italian in me, as if they told me, *Ah, you are Italian.* I felt inside that I had found something that just fit me, so I smiled at that remark.

The funny thing was also that I met the energy. It was like being back on track, like that energy I had been searching for all my life was here in Italy, and the whole group of Italians would lead me, in a way, so I felt really that this was a door to enter.

The seminar led me to friends and the friends later led me to a healing, but more about that in another chapter.

CHAPTER 6 • THE HELPING PEOPLE ARRIVE

You got a kundalini going on

The next seminar took me to Germany, and this seminar became one of those moments which turned everything around 180 degrees whenever I think about the kundalini.

I arrived there, and some of the Italians were there, so I felt a bit like family and all the fun we had, and Italy was there, too.

The first day of the seminar started. We were in this big room in Germany. There were big wooden houses and mountains, and I remember standing there. Everybody was excited about this big seminar; I think we were more than 60 people and I stood there next to a friend of mine, and the teacher walked up to us, he looks at me and then he says, "Ah, you've got a kundalini going on. You are going to have fun here."

I just looked at him. I was so stunned, and I was so surprised – first of all, that he could see it. He was glancing up and down my body, and I was thinking, *wow, how can he see that?*

It was also so amazing because I was so happy. Something that has been inside me for so long that I thought was so strange and so weird, and then to have someone just walk up to you and say, "Hey, you've got a kundalini going on." Him just seeing that without me telling him even a little about it made the kundalini very real.

I was also wondering what was going to happen these next four days.

Later that day, we were doing some body work on each other because this was a workshop where we were learning some of the techniques for the body work. He pressed very gently, hardly touching my back. The energy ran up the spine and made a reaction that stiffened the whole body. He said "Whoa," and I said "No!" really hard, because I was so surprised that just him touching me slightly could do that to the energy.

I also got really scared because I got this spasm of energy. It was like a spasm running up the spine. He said "No, it is okay. You do not have to do that."

I didn't want to go there, but at the same time I did want to go there because I wanted something to change really badly.

Later on in the day, I talked to the instructor and I said, "I am so scared of it and I do not know what is going to happen and I am scared that it is going to be so horrible again." He said, "it is better if you let it go."

I said that I was so scared it was going to trigger everything again and I was going to get really sick again, and he said he could understand that, but he said, "I am here, and it is okay to let go."

Then I left, and I thought about it and came back to him. I looked at him and said, "Can we make an agreement?"

He said, "Yes."

I said, "If I get scared in any way in the next three days, I can just call out your name and you will be there."

He said "Yes. I promise you, I will be there 100%."

I said, "Okay, I will let go."

He said "You have a deal."

The next day, we came to the workshop again, and we had to do some more body work on each other. I was lying down on the massage table; the masseuse was pressing one spot on my leg, and I just remember she was doing it over and over again.

I could just feel things started running now and just rise. The last thing I thought was, "I let go" and then the energy got completely wild. It was as if I let go of all the control I had been trying to hold inside my body.

I do not know what happened, but I was told afterwards that eight people were holding me in the air with this strong energy, and one guy that was really strong and was holding me said afterwards, "I have never felt so much power from such a small person." He said, "It was amazing, and I could barely hold you."

I was hanging up in the air and I just let the energy out. I knew the instructor was there, so I knew that everything was safe and I let go and I let go and I let go. I was out there, showing all my anxiety, all that I had been trying to control for so many years, and suddenly I hear, "Let her lie down now."

I was so tired. For the first time, I had relinquished all control, and I was completely spent. I went outside in the sun and sat down, and it was an amazing feeling that all this energy that I had been so scared of for so long was supported.

I remember also feeling that the energy of the Italians there made me feel safe. I didn't know why, but their presence made me dare to go there. For the first time, I was in this place where it was like looking your inner demon in your eyes, and I saw I didn't die and I didn't go crazy and I didn't lose it or anything.

When I left Germany, it was the first time in my life with kundalini that I felt it would not kill me, that even if it was still doing a lot of things, it would not kill me. I had never understood how scared I had been of this happening, that the kundalini could kill me.

I think maybe in a soul wave and a life wave and a body wave, it was a big relief to find that it could not mess me up in that way anymore.

Singapore

Something really changed after Germany. I suddenly felt I could be with the energy in a different way, so when it is burning it is like I can be more present with it.

I feel a bit friendlier with the energy, but it was still like a stranger inside me and it is still like a thing apart from myself. It is as if there is me and then there is the kundalini, so it is not a part of me. It is this energy within me.

A new seminar came up, and I was going with the energy again, looking at it, and I could just see I was going to the seminar, and it was in Singapore. I thought why on earth do I want to go to Singapore to take a four-day seminar, but I just had to go.

I took off, and I headed east. At this seminar, the teacher was talking about the kundalini. We were a small group. He was talking about his wife who had a kundalini and what she was going through. It was something about sleeping, that she was not sleeping at that time, and I could sort of mirror myself in that one.

Then he said something very important. He was telling us that the kundalini is not something you can get rid of. You have to live with it for the rest of your life. Then he talked about his own one, but that is not a disturbing one.

I just sat there, and it was as if like I couldn't understand what he was saying – that I had to live with this the rest of my life. I just picture the rest of my life with this horrible energy. The tears ran down my cheeks while I was sitting there in the room. I was devastated.

I had this dream that I could overcome it, that I could get rid of it, and now he was telling me that I had to live with it for the rest of my life. My hope and my wish that I could get rid of it so I could be happy with my life again vanished in that second.

In the break, he comes up and asked what happened, and I said I just understood that I can't get rid of it and I have this horrible one inside me. He approached it with a very kind energy and he understood me.

It was a deep sorrow that I had to face, that this was not something I could get rid of. Then I got angry with myself. I got angry with myself so badly, more than I had been before, that I had been the one wanting this.

As I wrote before, even if it was something that happened to me, I still felt I was the one who had asked for it. How can you ask for something that is so horrible towards your body and your soul and your family and everything? How could I do that, and how could my life ever be great again?

I had done this because I thought I could have a great life. Instead, I now had this and I felt that I was not to be trusted. I could not trust myself and that inner voice.

Looking back

I just distrusted that inner voice because it had let me down so badly, led me to this horrible place, but in a way that inner voice was also the one leading me to this life I should live, and that is myself.

I distrusted it and trusted it at the same time. If I didn't get the result exactly in that moment, if felt that I was distrusting it. I could also see the voice that was in me going to these places, actually helping me heal myself and getting closer to myself, so it was an ambiguous thing.

I felt I distrusted it because it had led me to a place where I didn't want to be, but I can also see that I trusted that voice by going to all these places that in a way didn't make sense.

I could see that listening to the voice made me go to places in the world, it made me dare to open up to people, and talk about this thing which I had thought had been so weird, an unreal thing, and picking the right people to help me heal, and they were there, and I sensed right. It was just a feeling I had when I was sensing the right people who could heal me.

My faith in never giving up was immensely big. I had this trust that I could heal, even though I didn't really trust it and was so scared. I also had this deep inner trust that I could get through it, and that was my stubbornness. I am so stubborn, and you can't tell me that I could not heal, that I should live this life that was so horrible.

I hoped that I would not have to be so hard on myself because it is a major job I performed, major work that I had gone through. I was so picky all the time that I could not do it in two weeks, but at that time it had taken me six or seven years to get to where I was.

On top of all the other things, being so hard on myself was the hardest to bear. I was punishing me beacuse it happened, because I could not get through it fast enough, because I needed other people, too – that was also a bad thing.

There were millions of things that just made me pick on myself all the time. Looking back, I wish that I had not been so hard on myself. I am also immensely grateful for all the people and teachers I have met who have helped me bit by bit getting healthier in my relationship with my kundalini.

CHAPTER 7
The tantric world

After Germany

I have written about all the sexual energy that was in my body all the time. Since I have met the Italians, some of my friends there were talking about it very openly, and that has been really nice.

I found it quite nice to talk with men about it; it felt much easier for me to talk about that strong ripping sexual energy and the feeling of a man entering me and making love to me in the weirdest situations all the time, to tell them that I could wake up in the middle of the night feeling that energy entering my body, and that I was constantly thinking about sex.

My mind was always in two places. I know they say you can only be in one place at a time, but I always felt I was in two.

Once I went to my therapist, the first one where it all happened. I had all this sexual energy. I was sitting there in the therapy session and I had all this desire. He asked, "Has it gone away?"

"No."

"Has it gone away?"

"No."

Basically, I was sitting there for an hour and it was there all the time. In the end I paid $120 for that, and it didn't help me. It didn't change anything.

After I had been in Germany, the instructor at the seminar said, "I have some files that can help you." I had not actually talked about the sexuality that much with him, but he said, "I have some audio files about kundalini," and I thought it was a lot of information about it. It was a whole bunch of audio files about sexual healing.

When I saw that, I understood that I had to do something. I really had to learn this energy, and how could I do that. I was tired of talking about it – the talking helped, it opened it up, but it was still in my body and I had no idea what to do with it.

I knew I needed to do something different and I needed to do something about it. I had a friend who recommended tantric massages.

I had been there once before, and I thought I had better go and check it out again. Even if I found it very weird, I know this place was known for being based on the old tantric philosophy, so I felt there was a bit more to it than just sexuality. There was a whole philosophy.

I decided when I came back from Germany to call them and ask for a massage. I was scared and nervous when I arrived. I was wondering what was going to happen, and how can I say this – a thousand thoughts entering. Also, the whole ambiance was so different from what I normally surrounded myself with.

I had a massage for the first time, and the person who was guiding me was completely calm about working with my kundalini and all my lust. He guided the energy, where to take it with my awareness, where to direct it. He guided me to open my heart towards it, and every time the energy would be too much and the anxiety was kicking in, he would guide me to breathe and to stay with the energy. To be with it rather than running away from it.

I think it is a strange world

For a long time, I just could not be at peace with myself all the times I walked through the door into the tantric world. I thought it was such a weird thing that I had to go through this door.

I had a hard time facing the reality of really needing this and that it was fantastic for me to be there. It was not so much about being in the massages that was weird, but it was going from my reality through that door that was such a huge step for me.

I struggled a lot with being so ashamed of having such strong sexuality. I was hiding myself, and I felt that something was wrong with me for having all this sexual energy. The masseur let me stay in this weirdness, and he also taught me to receive this beautiful energy, taught me that it is my life energy, that I have so much energy in my life and in my body and my soul. I should use it everywhere in the world. I must not suppress it but use it.

Bit by bit, I learn to breathe with it, be with it a bit more. I felt peace with that. The masseur could see that and helped me to expand it and start to really own the energy. In all these massages, I could cry, I could laugh, I could be anxious, I could be terrified, I could be loved, I was loving, I was spiritual, I was body, I was lust – I was everything – and I understood tantra, and that tantra was everything. My life energy, my kundalini, was everything.

It was not about all this sexual energy – it was about helping me open up for all this energy. It was not always pretty because all the locked up emotions were coming out when I was in the massages, I learned about myself little by little and became aware of who I was and what this energy was.

The power of the energy

In the massages, I started to learn to stay in my body while I got the massages. Every time the energy started shivering through my body and was going in all directions, he taught me to stop and observe what was happening so I didn't become the energy in the way that scared me, or tried to make it a third entity but just staying with it, feeling it in my body and at the same time starting to be really aware of it – where I felt it, how it felt, how I could breathe within it, how I could stay with it without running away and detaching myself from it.

I had been running for such a long time from this moment, and I could see that the more I had run away from it, the stronger it got. The gap between kundalini and me had become bigger and stronger. Right now, I was learning to stay in the present with the energy and not run.

I started to see that when I could stay with it, it could stay with me, and I stopped running from me. Slowly I accepted that all this sexual energy was just a mirror of me. It was my life energy, and I was born with a lot of energy. I have a lot of energy which is also reflected in my sexual energy, and hence it is also reflected in me having so much kundalini energy. By slowly realizing that this energy was not some third phenomenon, or someone else, but that it was me and my energy, I learned something very important from it, and that was directing it. I had been trying to close down all this energy and trying to control it, but it was still there.

The tantric massages were not just about having this sexual energy up through all the chakras and up through my heart and up to the neck and up in the brain and crown chakra, it was also that I could use this energy in any area in my life.

If I really wanted to do something in my job, just direct the energy right there. It was all about directing the energy that suddenly made me be in charge of my life. It was not running me, I was running it.

When kundalini woke me up, I was this flood of energy, just like a river flooding its banks. Now that I could start seeing that I could use all this water, all this energy, I could direct it in different ways so the water would go to small rivers and I could say, "I need the energy here and I need it there."

In the massages, we also talked a lot about what was happening at the same time, so when I had the sensation, we talked. Every time I was anxious, I could put words to it and I could work my way through it so as to become aware of it.

If I got sad, there was space in the room for nurturing that. It was healing, so healing. All this sexual energy I had been walking around with, all the while trying to suppress it, I finally started to accept, and it started to blossom within me.

At this time, I also started to meditate. I meditate every morning. This was to give this calmness and, again, discipline. I have to be disciplined so I can freely be focused where the energy must go in my life. Otherwise, it becomes a huge flood of all this energy again.

I am very aware of being very disciplined about where the energy should go.

God

I slowly started to feel this connection on every level of me in the massages. It was not just about my body and my sexuality. It was not just about my heart. It was about love, the universe. The massage became greater and greater. In the beginning, it was just the suppressed sexual energy, and then I worked through that and directed the energy and love and the awareness.

The God came my way. He didn't come in in person, of course, or anything like that, but it was a very special feeling. I was having my massage when I suddenly burst into tears because I was so longing to get home to God.

I suddenly felt and understood the separation I had subjected myself to. I separated myself from God, from love, from everything around me. In fact, everything was here and now, and I had separated myself from God so much because I was not brought up in such a way that I could talk about God as being a part of my world.

In the massages, I know that people think a lot about the tantric, that it is just about sexuality, but suddenly my awareness was raised so much because the energy had direction now, and I suddenly came into this huge experience where I felt that I was one with everything and one with God and God was within me.

That was an immense and fantastic experience to have.

Healing the weeting of my inner man and woman

I also became quite aware of my picture of the man and the woman that I had been longing to heal. In many ways, it was becoming so clear to me that part of the tantric world is that the masculine side is the awareness, the direction whereas the feminine side is all the energy.

When these two merge, they can accomplish big things. With the massages, I started to merge those parts of me – the female and the masculine side – and it was the picture I had of the man and woman, and I thought it had to be an outer man, but I always knew that I had to heal it within myself.

For me, it was time to receive them both within me, as if they had become lovers within me, supporting each other, melting into each other. It was that love I was seeking and had been looking for all the time, that deep universal love and love of God, of myself and of everything inside me.

It was like the merging of two drops that melt together and become one. The water had been so dirty for such a long time, but now I could start seeing clearly how I was coming home.

Love, love, love – It hurts to open my heart

One of the great things about my tantric journey was learning to love. I know that it can be very misunderstood, that tantric is just about the sexuality, but tantra is actually about the whole energy system, and also about using our sexual energy and our life energy to bring it up higher in the body and be aware of the energy of opening up the heart and, in the full state, to open up to being more conscious in life, to gain more consciousness.

My whole journey with kundalini had been learning to love – this quest to learn how to love. I saw this, as I have written above, the inner man and the inner woman. The tantric journey helped me open up the heart. Because I became more and more aware of all the kundalini energy, I could more consciously bring it up in my energy system and follow it by being aware of it.

The masseuse helped me to get into one of these blocks where the energy stopped in my body.

For me, it became about setting my heart free – to love and dare to love, to tell people that I love – but I was just not used to that. I was not used to telling someone that I loved them without me wanting something in return. For me, suddenly I realized that loving someone unconditionally sounds so easy but is so damn hard to practice and maybe it's even a cliché that if you don't love like that you don't truly love. It killed my heart many, many times. Because I had the tantric journey with me, I could constantly come back in that energy where it was okay to open up and show the world my love and my heart.

That helped me heal myself because the energy of opening up the heart made the energy go from the lower chakras, and all the stuck sexual energy that was constantly going around like a washing machine in my lower sexual chakra helped bring it up to feeling God and feeling the higher purpose and being more conscious with the energy.

Not being suppressed anymore helps my energy, and it helps me to not long for this deep, deep love of the outer world. I travel to places where I can learn to love.

I was still not where I felt kundalini and where I became one with it all the time, but I felt that my anxiety at having this energy within me was not so big anymore, and the more I had these long massages and the more I learned the energy, the more she became my lover.

It was my energy that I was making love with. It was not a terrifying monster within me. It was as if she became more and more like someone I could face without fear.

I remember one time that was very strong for me when I was in the massage, and I let the energy sort of make love to me. I was moving myself and my body just where the energy was, and it was like a sensual dance with myself where the masseuse was just observing me in this energy.

From that moment, kundalini became my lover, and there was a nurturing and a kindness in the energy that I had not been able to receive before, and hence the drama and the anxiety and the torture was starting to melt.

Looking back

I know that sexuality is a very sensitive matter, and we are very drawn to it because it is our instinct. When talking about sexuality and spirituality, it can often end up as two opposites, and we wonder what they have to do with each other?

When we talk about spirituality, we always talk about the wholeness and the oneness, but still there are often parts we do not want to include. Because we prefer to see spirituality as this beautiful world of light and love. We tend to disregard the negative aspects such as anger, anxiety, sadness, and sex. To me, spirituality is the whole thing, and sexuality is also a part of it. We must include ALL.

I am very grateful to have met the tantric world that could guide me through this journey; it helped heal me ever so much.

The whole tantric world taught me how to stop running away from my energy – from myself – and instead teach myself who I really am, how to contain my life energy and use it instead of dividing it, throwing it away, closing my eyes, and disowning it.

I understood that the picture I had seen of the man and the woman since the beginning of this Kundalini journey was this picture of myself, of the freedom within me and the truth within me, of my inner marriage, and I was healing it now.

It was not just about loving others or loving myself, but it was that inner feeling of universal love.

I have read books later on about kundalini, and they talk about a lot of sexual energy, but the feeling of being so violated by it is not really discussed. I think it is because we are scared of seeing the whole thing as just an energy and realizing why we have it and why such a strong sexual sensation comes with the kundalini. But that is just my point of view.

It is because it is our life energy. This, and the tantric philosophy, helped me to bring up the energy and make it my energy. For me, that is a very beautiful aspect of the tantric world. It is about the heart. It is about opening up our hearts and opening up to be more loving towards ourselves, our bodies, our hearts, our souls and God and the universe and everyone around us.

It brought me back home a long way. I helped me. It was fantastic to meet it, and I am grateful that I never gave up on the picture I had of the man and the woman because staying focused on that image kept me on track and made me meet the people who could help heal me very deep within.

CHAPTER 8
My Italian angel

Rome, I love you

I met the Italians on that seminar in Italy close to Venice. I had this very strong urge to go back to Italy, and suddenly there came a seminar in Rome and I just knew I had to go there. I packed my stuff once again and headed south towards Rome.

It was an amazing feeling because I was sitting in the airplane, and the moment we landed on the runway, there was something in my body saying, *Wow, I am home!* I never had that feeling in my whole life before. I never had that feeling of belonging somewhere.

Suddenly, just by some wheels landing in Rome, I felt home. That amazed me so much. It was so strong in my body, but I also thought that was a really weird thing. I need to learn why I feel like this.

I went to the seminar. It was great, and I hooked up with all my friends again. I was in Rome. I had half a day before the seminar started a bit outside Rome.

First I went down to the hotel reception and asked the receptionist how I could get around in Rome, and he asked if I liked to walk. I said that I loved to walk, so he said you go there and there and there. Nothing is very far in Rome.

I took the bus and went to the Coliseum tube station. I will never forget when I walked up the stairs and saw the Coliseum. It was so magnificent. That day, I walked and walked and walked around. I was so amazed and I was so in love with this feeling so at home in this amazing architecture and history and the very vibes of Rome. I had it all in my body.

I went back and had the seminar, and then I went home again. I knew a new chapter in my life had just begun, because I had to go back to Rome, and I wondered what made me feel so connected with the place Why is it this feeling so stron? I could not understand it and I could not explain it to anyone. I just knew I had to go. The urge was so strong that I simply had to go.

I had such a hard time explaining to other people why I had to go. I said I need to write down there. That was sort of my excuse for going there because just to say I needed to go to Rome sounded a bit vague, at least to myself, and to begin with.

I started traveling to Rome every month. I needed to be there. It was as if my body was screaming for it, for walking down the streets of Rome. It was just about drinking my cappuccino in Rome, it was about eating, walking by the sea, listening to the sea. It had a different sound there. Everything had a different smell. I felt part of the city, on a very huge scale.

I went to see churches. I lit candles in the churches. It was just about being there. It was a very odd feeling that every time I went there and went back home after a week, I felt something had changed in me, so I knew it was very important, even if I hadn't done anything but eating and walking around.

The transforming oil bath angel arrives

I had a common interest with a friend in Rome, and it was all about this quest of living from my heart, peeling off the dirt and just live truthfully from my heart. There were many ways we were practicing that with sessions and different kinds of workshops that would lead us there.

One of them was making an oil bath, which my friend could do, and that was making a special plan to cleanse parts of his soul. I had been in Rome, and he took some of my hairs and asked me if I wanted to have this oil bath. I said yes, sure, that would be great, I would like that.

CHAPTER 8 • MY ITALIAN ANGEL

I wrote down something and said okay, that is cool and went back home and called him up and asked him, "what about this oil bath?" He said he would make it. He analyzed what it was he was doing, and he came up with a special oil for me: what I needed was jasmine oil.

It turned out to be quite a journey for the jasmine to reach me, since there were a lot of posting problems from Italy. When it finally got to my home, it had taken a month for this oil to arrive. And as a special irony, I decided I would go to Rome again, and I ended up taking the oil there.

I was lucky to get the only room in the hotel with a bathtub. This jasmine oil had become a big thing. There was something magic about taking this bath because it had taken so long to get the oil. I was going into this very humble mood in the evening where I lit all the candles in the bathroom, I put on some music. I filled the tub with very hot water and I had all the ingredients for this bath. It needed some crystals and salts, and it was a very relaxing ambiance when I entered the water.

I finally put the golden drops of jasmine in the water. I went down underneath the water. You have to keep yourself completely under water, and I struggled a bit with that in the beginning. I had a very hard time to relax, but finally I felt some peace within me in this hot water with the music and the candlelight. I started to receive this feeling of lying down.

Suddenly, I saw someone. I saw the face quite clearly. And saw that it was a he. I could see his dark hair, brown eyes and his face, his very round, warm head.

Who was this? This was the first time I was not scared of the dead, because I have seen shadows for many years, but I have always felt like saying, *stay away from me, I do not want you here*. This time, I didn't feel that anxiety.

I asked, "Who are you?"

And he told me his name.

I said "What?"

He said, "Yes, I am your friend's brother," and I knew it was true. I have never seen a picture of his brother. I just knew that my friend's brother had died some years ago.

I asked, "Why are you here? Why have you come to me?"

He replied, "Because you love my brother the way I do and I know you would never claim to possess him." The weird thing was this was so natural, that he was there and I was just lying there. He said I should tell his brother that I love him. I just thought, no way. It is okay with me that I do, but I do not need the misunderstanding of this "I love you" kind of thing. Nobody said you have to open and strengthen your heart, you have to expand. Everything was good the way it was.

I had to tell his brother that things were good the way they were and I had to tell him that this was a message to him and he thinks that he should receive me for him and I just had this love for him and he should not be scared anymore and he should start writing.

And then he disappeared.

What? What was that? I waited until the clock rang for my bath because I had to be in there for 20 minutes. The second it rang, I thought I needed to write this down. I went and took a pen and I wrote all this down.

I wrote down who he was. I just wrote that he is really sweet, he is laughing, incredible, a massive heart and just this very deep frequency in his heart.

I woke up the next day. That day, I was supposed to leave back home again. I was doing some work with my friend and I was not concentrating because I had to tell him this.

I said, "I need to tell you something," and I told him what happened with the bath.

He said, "Whoa!" and put his hands to his face. I don't know why I was so scared of this moment. He said it had happened before, that his brother had come to other people so it was not the first time, and I felt a bit relieved with this.

Suddenly, I had an angel in my life.

CHAPTER 8 • MY ITALIAN ANGEL

Can I say no to an angel?

He was there all the time. When I flew back home, he was sitting there. He was there in the plane. He was giggling, he had fun. He was constantly talking. He wanted to hear music. I saw myself putting music on that I had no idea why I wanted to listen to.

It was very surreal and very real at the same time. How could I say no to this? This was my beloved friend's brother. Suddenly, I was in a very odd situation. I was in a deep sorrow between two brothers who had a very special bond and this very deep brother love, and they were in each their world now.

Up till now, the whole travel had been about opening up my heart and loving and being loved, and now I was here with an angel, loving him. My heart was putting on a completely new experience and it was being challenged.

The fear that was in me was reflected outside. I felt that I was challenged all the time.

I took a trip to Thailand to visit a therapist and the author of a book about love. That book really touched me because he could write about love in this non-possessive way. Most books are about relationships and how we can make them work and what to do.

Here was a book written about the energy, love, that it is here all the time and we just have to open our hearts to receive it and we can't own this one. It was the first time someone had written something that I felt so acquainted with. It was something that was really me talking.

I went over there to visit him, and I felt I was sitting with a person who understood that when we just love fully from our hearts, we can merge with each other and become this light that I had seen with kundalini, so for me this book was part of this bigger understanding in the journey of kundalini.

This inner state I had, this inner picture I had about love, felt like it was there with me, I could meet that in life and I could travel with someone to do that with the same understanding of it. Before I had wanted someone out there to show it to me, and now I knew it was my journey to find it within myself first.

Anyway, we were sitting in northern Thailand one evening, and I told the author about this angel. She said to me, "you can always say you do not want them there," and that triggered something in me because I felt I could not say no to him. I felt that was a bigger learning for me and I knew she was so right. I could say no, but I was just not prepared at that moment to do so.

I also felt that I wanted to do it for my friend but at the same time I was not feeling safe, I was not feeling peaceful with whether he wanted this. It was about me feeling more relaxed within this.

The following night, I was extremely restless the whole night, and I was not happy at all. I was thinking about the whole situation with the angel, and I wanted to set him free.

He said it was not really my decision to make, that I should just feel peace and stay and open my heart and just show him that love was not so scary. I felt the angel had this very deep warm frequency in his heart, and his unconditional love was just beaming out. He was really teaching me. I felt that when he was around and present, my heart could just expand and expand and I felt loving. I learned so much. For him, just being there was his energy and his presence.

I was lying in bed the whole night and felt him, and I thought that this was my decision, my choice if I wanted this. He lay down in bed with me, and I felt more peace. He said, "It is okay."

In the late hours, I finally closed my eyes in this very peaceful land of northern Thailand with an angel in my bed.

My body started really to burn again

The trip to Rome was very important. I really felt the angel and Rome itself healed me.

For a long time I had felt okay with the burning in my body and the

CHAPTER 8 • MY ITALIAN ANGEL

sensation and the kundalini; I just felt more at ease with everything.

One evening at home, things started to light up in my spine again, and I was feeling really bad. I got really scared again. I was in a panic. I thought *oh, no, not again. I am going to lose it again now,* and all these old memories were coming up. It had been such a long time since it was so bad.

I called a practitioner, and she asked me if I was sure this was not kundalini stuff going on again. I said, yes, I know. She told me to try to call this woman in the States. She has been through the same as you. So I did.

For the first time, I met someone in a conversation about kundalini who had been through it herself and to the same degree as myself. She knew all about the sexual sensation, the anxiety, all the burning. All the sensations I had, she had them too. She knew the fear of losing your mind.

It was not so much about the practical things she could do, but her understanding was a huge gift. She said to me that this energy is you and you have to live it. Every time something feels wrong in your life, you have to change it. You have to do something about it, otherwise you will always stir up your body because she is just there reminding you of you.

I had probably been told this before. I felt it before, but when she said it, I understood it from really deep within me that I had to choose her. I had to live by kundalini's will, and I had been fighting it. By fighting it, I had been fighting myself, fighting the way that I am living and she is just really showing my way.

This became a major shift in my life because suddenly when I made decisions, I made them from this big perspective of me, her, and I didn't have to explain it to anyone. I always wanted to explain it and get someone to agree with me so they understood where I was coming from.

By completely listening to myself, I understood what I had done before when I was really bad. I had to do this non-stop in my life; otherwise, she will stir up my body and my mind until I choose her.

The rest of it

I understood now that this was about really listening to myself and that I could not avoid making this journey. The journey was already there for me, and even if it changes all the time, it is like having different purposes in life that can also change. I just had to listen to that voice in me all the time and, more importantly, obey it.

All kundalini, my life energy, wanted to show me was just that. For the first time, kundalini became more female for me, not this aggressive one, but she became soft and nurturing for me.

It was not about living according to specific rules in my life. It was about living out what had already been given me from birth and I should not listen to the outer rules of the right or the wrong ways but listen to what I should do in life from that purpose within me. Really, she was a huge gift for me because she could tell me when I was not on track with myself.

I feel I fail in unconditional love

The hardest part was that I constantly felt I was failing in just loving, because on the way to opening up my heart, a lot of all the dirt I was cleansing came up and I could see that there were parts of me where I was not that clean in loving.

At the same time, I knew it was a journey to open up my heart, and it was teaching me to be with that clean love, but on the way, all the unclean stuff came up, and that hurt.

It hurt that I had to go through it and transform it. I just wanted to love actively and unconditionally with no strings attached. For a long time I felt like I could deal with them myself and I could deal with them with people I could share this with so I can state loving actively someone who you do not love in a way that you should have some.

I wanted to learn how to love. Every time I felt I got struggled with things that got stuck, I told myself that I had to love even more. The whole journey of teaching myself to love actively felt like one big failure.

I felt that one day, I should come to a point where I ought to get a medal or whatever, but it is not like that in love. God does not show up with a medal and tell you that you did so well.

I had for a very long time felt so embarrassed about loving, and felt the embarrassment of loving someone you should not be with. It has taken me a long time to understand why that should be embarrassing because so many people believe we should live from our hearts, we should express our love in this loving world - peace and love in the world.

A part of that also has to do with daring to tell to people you meet on your way that you love them, and sharing that with them. Not for them to give it back to you, but daring to open up.

I just feel I failed and failed, over and over again, and every time I was met with anger, anxiety, or when I felt like running away or felt that I looked like an idiot, I didn't know what to do, how to do . . . but somehow, I stayed.

Looking back

When I look back at this chapter in my life, I am quite amazed that I did this because it was a very hard time for me. I felt I was living in this space of no direction, and there was a direction all the time.

Emotionally, it was very hard for me to have this connection between two brothers. At the same time, it also taught me so much about love. Looking back, I wish I could just have accepted it more and just been in it instead of trying to understand it or trying to explain it to others.

I feel that we have all be given a life, and the more we listen to that life which has been given to us, the easier it is just to follow life and go through it instead of getting stuck, and the more direction you can get where it is unfolding. Looking back at this period of my life, a lot of magic was unfolding, but I was just not willing to see the magic there. I felt it was hard because the love and the search and the quest for love was so big that I accepted it and did it because I do things that do not make sense.

Rome became a very big lesson for me. I was extremely amazed at receiving this information from an angel.

I think it was hard because he pushed me, but in a good way because he pushed me out there and showed me love, and this angel had love that was so big.

We may talk endlessly about living love from the heart, set up special conditions, do anything, really, but this is not love. Loving is something that we can do actively. By doing that, it is not just words.

It can be expressed in many ways, and sometimes it is to leave a situation and sometimes it is to stay in a situation and show people that you see them. Sometimes seeing them is also seeing yourself, and seeing from a bigger perspective that love is here all the time and is really just about receiving love and opening up for it.

CHAPTER 9

I am coming home

It was time to make a closure

I love the quote from Krishnamurti:

"It is the truth that liberates, not your effort to be free."

In that moment where you are really willing to look at the truth, things are set free. Something happened suddenly in Rome. I was willing to see and express all that love, no matter if the consequences were that I should not hold on to Rome, or hold on to anything.

It was that greater love, the bigger perspective, but also understanding that this is not something to be explained or to be lived; in that moment it was like releasing the truth with a witness. Sometimes it is nice to have a witness even though it is a breakdown or releasing of the truth.

In that moment, I understood my journey to Rome and why it had been so important. It had been a mixture of Rome and my friend and the angel. I also understood that when I came back from that trip, I had released something. I had seen the whole picture and I knew that the travel, the journey to Rome, was about to end.

I got back to my home in Rome. I had been in that house for some time. I cleansed the house. That evening, I was sitting alone. I had some candles there. I felt the whole place was at peace and I felt I was peaceful, so in a way I felt that we were ending mutually. I fell fully at home.

I went to my bed and the angel arrived. I was sitting in my bed, and it was completely dark in the room. He sat just in front of me.

I said to him, "I am leaving now."

He said, "I know, and it is okay."

For the first time, he let go. There was just this fantastic love between us. I let go, and he let go.

The next morning, I woke up and packed my stuff. In a split second, I just knew that now it was the time to leave. I felt very calm about the situation, even if it had been a long journey. I felt a deep inner peace.

I knew that the next time I would come it was because I had to pack up my stuff and send it home.

When I went to the airport, I sent a text message to my dear friend in Denmark, and I wrote her, "I am coming home." It was a very strong message for me to send because for the first time I actually felt that flying home to my own country was like flying home.

That was a huge change.

I am going home

I was at the airport, and the plane was about to take off. I was ready to go because I felt there was nothing left to learn. The knowledge had been found and it was in my heart and my soul now.

In a way it was a relief that this constant *why am I here?* found its closure then, and I really felt like I was going home now, and I was at home with myself. That was a huge change that came suddenly. I didn't have to fly around to find myself. I was here with me, no matter where I was. I was home because I was with me.

I felt this journey had been a mess. I felt the way I had communicated love had probably been wrong. The way I did it was not perfect, and I just felt completely imperfect in the way I loved.

That in itself had been a huge journey because I thought that when you loved unconditionally, it would be this perfect way of doing it with calm and ease… but it was not. It had been a mess, and it was a mess inside me and the way I communicated had been a mess, but I learned it. It was a spiritual challenge for me, and the whole journey had been really about finding myself and loving myself from a very deep place within. I had this illusion about spiritual awakening, and that I had to be more detached from things in that mess, but the whole way of acknowledging that was not that easy.

Many people say that you have this kundalini and you get all enlightened, but I think this is a huge misunderstanding. I had to face a mess all the time, and I also had to face that, in fact, I became more and more human in the way of this waking myself up with all this life energy.

This is one of the great insights that I have gained for myself and my body. I love my body and all that makes me human because I am not supposed to be anything but a human.

As free persons, we are everything.

This is me sitting in the airplane, me relaxed in my seat, flying home, and for the first time not feeling *when should I go back again?* but just feeling the ease and peace of going home.

Love and peace

When I sat there, understanding that this journey had been about this masterpiece of work that I have done, the soul work for me and feeling the love for myself, I saw that because I loved Rome, the angel had taught me how to love. Loving on such a scale had reflected back on me and I was now here with this great love.

I was not perfect. I was a diamond full of flaws, but even the flaws were fantastic. I understood that I didn't have to be something I was not. I had to embrace the love towards myself, the love I was.

I understood that the life I was going to live now should be lived in respect of who I am and then things will fall into place, even if you have to go through things that hurt, it will still fall into place on a bigger scale. I tried so long to fit in, and the only thing I really needed to fit in was me.

It was as if life was turned upside-down and everything fell into place that day. I felt like an inner puzzle had come together. I didn't feel that I was a thousand pieces anymore. I felt whole for a while.

I had made a great journey and met with great love. For the first time I felt a huge gratitude towards myself for all I had done to heal myself; because I had not gone crazy and because I hadn't been sitting still and refrained from doing the things I had done, all of which were needed for me to heal. I had not really thanked myself before that, simply because I always felt I didn't do enough and that what I did was never good enough.

That was one of the hardest parts also that the whole journey was that I had not been choosing the things for me before. Now I saw that my body just could not allow that anymore. It was not possible.

This was also the most loving part of the whole kundalini journey. It helps me to live as who I am because I am simply not allowed to do anything else. It is that honesty and truthfulness towards myself which does not match with any illusion about life and how I want to live it.

I have to be completely truthful with me. Even though this is something that used to annoy me for so long that I could not live by it, it basically annoyed me because I didn't really think that my life would be great if I was me.

I guess with this inner fight, I really didn't want to be me because I didn't like me – I didn't love me. I thought I was weird. I thought I was strange. I just wanted to be normal. I just wanted to be like everyone else.

That made my kundalini much worse because I was blocking my own energy. I didn't want to accept that this energy was *me*. I felt that I lost control of the life I wanted and had planned to live.

It took me a very long time to really listen to my inner voice, and at the same time, I have done everything I thought I should not do, but I did it anyway. I had listened, but I had not paid attention, and I have not been happy about it.

Probably this becoming awake and being enlightened is a big thing, and a lot of people are trying to achieve it, but for me the awakening part has been about awakening myself and my soul. There is no right way to do that, and I had misunderstood that quite a lot.

CHAPTER 9 • I AM COMING HOME

I have peeled down to all these illusions I feel to exist about the awakening part, especially about the kundalini. It is about bringing that down to earth and see it for what it is and make it more human instead of making it more of an illusio, really, because it is a part of me – me being human.

CHAPTER 10
Wrapping up

The sensations are still here

Even though I have come a very long way, now that I am writing this book, I still have to learn, and I will have that feeling until I die. I still have sensations like burning or feeling that the energy is pulling me down to the ground and sometimes making me so dizzy I need to rest.

I need a lot of discipline – eat well, exercise, treat myself, meditate in the morning to make things go well. I know now when something is disturbing it is because of the stuff I do not really deal with. I have to look at it in a wider perspective. I have to look at it, and I have to see what is.

I use it to increase my awareness about myself, about the present moment, about the truth about me, about the truth about my relationship, and it has become a guide to what I have to choose to be full of me, what is stopping me, and what is blocking me from becoming more than I am.

I do not fight it anymore, and I accept that it has happened to me. Just those two things are a huge step because it does not block the energy. There was a man with whom I walked in the woods, and one day he said to me, "Why do you fight your natural gifts?"

I replied that I didn't really want this kundalini, and he said many people are desperate to receive all this you have been given and all these gifts you have – your sensitivity, your understanding, your special sensing. You have come by this so easily, and then you just fight it and want to get rid of it. I felt a bit like a spoiled kid when he said that. In a way, it was good that he told me, because I understood that I had been fighting my nature.

I should receive this is a gift and as a blessing instead of as a curse. It is a true gift.

I still get sessions to help me unblock and become more aware all the time as my life unfolds; I am human and I have my bumps on the road, I need discipline. As I said, I need to live out of my body and my mind and soul all the time. I am much more sensitive to that than others.

Sometimes I get jealous that people can just shut off from all this, and I can be quite amazed that they can do it, because I cannot. At the same time, I am very grateful it is like that because it means I live me.

It is still here, it is just very different and I feel much more at peace with the whole thing.

Accepting what is

Accepting what is. It sounds so easy. It sounds so fantastic – just tune in and out.

I think this is hard to practice in real life, and it has been hard for me to accept what I have been given. I sometimes tell myself that I am accepting it, but it is crap. It has been hard to accept that I am not mainstream – I am different.

It is a quality and it is an amazing one, but accepting my life as it is, accepting me and who I am is a long process. The kundalini has helped me to accept it because in many ways it has barred me from choosing not to accept. It has compelled me to accept and use all the gifts I have and to open up to awareness instead of finding it wrong or strange or weird.

I also accept that I have a very sensitive awareness which gives me access to much more information than meets the eye. I use it in my everyday life now, but I no longer get overwhelmed by it in the same way as before. Often it is more like eating my dinner. Sometimes it feels as if heaven has come down to earth.

CHAPTER 10 • WRAPPING UP

It does not always have to be something extraordinary. It is just what it is. It is my energy, my life energy and it is the kundalini. It is not fancier than anything else. It has often been hell and at such times, I would gladly have sold it or given it to anyone for the asking.

I do not understand why some people really want this and when I hear about people who meditate for years to achieve it, because I think there are so many illusions about it. Now I see more people who have it, and they are like me, so I am quite amazed that some people really want this.

Then again, as is my point, it is a journey.

I tried everything to make it go away – tried to neglect it. It has been a very big part of my life which I had to deal with. I still have to deal with it, but, then again, I also deal with everyone around me when I cook, wake up in the morning, get dressed, clean, or work. What makes me feel alive, really, is just being a human being.

It has been a long and arduous trip since 2004 when I was 32 years old to get the energy down on the ground. I feel that it is so much more grounded now, and it is grounded in my body. It is not so significant now, so I no longer have to deal with it on such a massive scale as before, but it is still my everyday life.

It is the same thing but with a different perspective now.

Looking back

The truth: seeing what is, is really the one factor that healed me all along; that, and being 100% honest about my truth. Every time I was stuck, it was because I had not been truthful – I mean, in detail. I can't lie, because when I do I get sick. When I'm not willing to see and feel myself, I get sick.

There are no shortcuts, and I have spent a lot of time explaining instead of changing. I felt that if I could explain it and talk about it, I could escape the truth. Every time I looked truth in the eyes, I see that this is where I was transformed. The truth heals.

I see that all the meetings were just love – daring to love myself, daring to love the ones I love without having to find or express a right solution for that love. I perceive that ability to be magical. I realize that this is what helped me so much.

I think it is amazing to see how much love can do when we dare to just really love; how much it can transform us and teach us a lot about life.

I have replaced all my former attempts at controlling the energy and holding it down with good discipline concerning living. I used to fight discipline. I hated it. I needed more discipline than a lot of other people – discipline about eating, exercising, sleeping, meditating – but I see that this is actually the main source of feeding myself with good energy. It is an amazing thing. For me, discipline has become a very positive thing in my life.

I had this illusion about becoming this peaceful person who could just be in my own state of mind all the time, but I am not that person. I am a mother, I am a lover, I am a woman, I am angry, I am wrong sometimes, I am crying, I am sensitive, I am loving. I am all this mess.

The ultimate lesson in all this is how to accept the freedom to be all that and receive it with my whole energy as I truly am.

I gave up being a seeker. I was tired. I was always trying to be more than I am. It was as if it was always wrong to be me and I always had to look for something better. I felt that I was not a good human being as I was.

When I stopped seeking, I stopped explaining myself all the time, explaining how I felt and why things were as they were, but eventually, it gave me space to exist in all this lovely mess. Life is messy. It is as it should be and that is the way it is.

For many people, it has become a goal to become enlightened, and this may be the right way for some people, but why do we suppose it to be the highest goal? The highest goal is to live as all these different souls we really are, but that used to confuse me a lot in the awakening process, and it kept me from being completely truthful; from going the way that was there for me and being the person that was me.

I wanted this clean energy so I could receive the awareness I had, and I think that has been one of the keys for me.

The whole journey of the kundalini is like taking something from heaven and bringing it down to earth so we can share the greater world together.

Looking back, I see there is no set direction for a kundalini journey. All journeys are unique because life is unique; every life is unique and every life energy is unique.

There are some similar traits that we can share and help each other with. But there is not only one way. There is not only one truth.

And that, in itself, is beautiful!

Postscript

As I said, I haven't been to India, but you know, life changes and who am I to say what is to come? One day the idea entered my mind, and within hours I had booked a trip to the place. I had no clue what was or what to expect, I only knew it said OSHO Meditation Center on my booking. I hadn't read about OSHO, I knew vaguely that I thought it would suit me, and that vague notion was right.

You see, the beauty of life is that I travel through life now, listening to that voice which is telling me what to do, where to go, what to heal, whom to kiss, whom not to kiss, what to eat, how to love, etc. I don't argue with it anymore, that chapter is closed. Kundalini is me and it's not scary anymore.

I have been opposed by people trying to awaken the kundalini through meditation, and I have thought that most people do not know what they are dealing with. Hence, when arriving in India, I got a bit nervous because it said OSHO Kundalini Meditations in the program.

I was nervous when it started but must say the meditations were so well put together, and I saw they were safe. Safe because they were not meditations designed to awaking kundalini. I have had the mildest and most wonderful state of being with these meditations.

I'm close with kunda now, we are one. And I am grateful for that inner knowledge that it has shown me that I'm in love with me. Love with all the healing it had brought me. The fight is over, the creative force has taken over and I'm ready for it to continue.

Stay grounded, don't force it, let it come if it's meant to be… And trust that being fully truthful is the way to go.

Kundalini is a mystery and it is real when it happens. I'm grateful to have received this journey, but not until now. Now, 13 years after I set out, I can laugh when writing that I once thought I could make the journey in a couple of months.

Enjoy yourself and your journey, we are only here once. Give it your all!

Follow me at my blog lottefarranlee.com

Email: l@lottefarranlee.com